SELLING GOLF

Ron Thatcher

GV979.C6 T53 2008
0134110993513

Thatcher, Ron.

Selling golf

c2008.

2008 09 03

© Copyright 2008 Ron Thatcher.
All rights reserved. No part of this publication may be reproduced, stored in a retrieval system, or transmitted, in any form or by any means, electronic, mechanical, photocopying, recording, or otherwise, without the written prior permission of the author.

ISBN 1-4196-8849-9

10 9 8 7 6 5 4 3 2 1

This book is dedicated to:

My wife, Gina

My daughters, Jordan, Loren and Taylor

My sales job can be incredibly simple or it can be endlessly complex. It can also be at times maddening and frustrating, at others joyous and fulfilling. This game of mental chess deals with the creative mind of the human being and all of the variables that come with it. The highs of a good streak touch the heavens while the lows of a bad one leave you perplexed. The thick skin of the sales professional leads us to strive to find the ultimate path around NO and ultimately enhance the age-old art of selling. This persuasive trade may be the greatest job ever created by man.

Ron Thatcher

Contents

Chapter 1	Introduction	1
Chapter 2	The History of Golf	4
Chapter 3	The Doctor	14
Chapter 4	How the System Works	19
Chapter 5	Golf Coach Planner	22
Chapter 6	The Language of Sales	33
Chapter 7	How to Speak to a Guest	35
Chapter 8	The Golf Orientation Trial	42
Chapter 9	The Golf Orientation Card	46
Chapter 10	My One on One Golf Presentation	49
Chapter 11	My Personal Coaching Script	53
Chapter 12	Introduction to the Prescriptive Presentation	56
Chapter 13	The Seven Steps to a Professionally Structured Golf Coaching Program	58
Chapter 14	Prescriptive Price Grid	60
Chapter 15	The Fisherman	62
Chapter 16	How and When to *T.O.*	66
Chapter 17	Filling Out the Golf Coaching Agreement	69
Chapter 18	How to Overcome Objections	74
Chapter 19	Closing	77
Chapter 20	My first experience as a coach and the Bobby Jones Story	103
Chapter 21	Helping your potential clients know that they don't know	116
Chapter 22	Time Management	121
Chapter 23	Personal Pro-lesson Re-signs	124

Selling Golf

Chapter 24 Master Appointment Book 127
Chapter 25 Working the Fairways.. 130
Chapter 26 The Wall of Fame 133
Chapter 27 The Closeout Master Plan 136
Chapter 28 Interacting with the Staff....................................... 141
Chapter 29 Giving a free Gift with Purchase.......................... 148
Chapter 30 Confirming Appointments and Cancellations 150
Chapter 31 Drilling 153
Chapter 32 The Sales Professional's Code 157
Chapter 33 To Sell or Not to Sell... 160

Chapter 1

INTRODUCTION

Welcome to *Selling Golf!!!* This book will offer the golf coach or golf professional an amazing opportunity to understand and master the business side of golf. If you are ready to stop struggling and start producing, then get ready to enjoy the first book that has ever been written using the actual techniques coveted by the top golf coaches in this growing industry.

This book will introduce you to the techniques that have built some of the largest, most successful training programs throughout the world. The golf industry's top producers have kept these proven techniques secret for decades. The material contained within this book has been tested, tried and retested before being implemented to produce outstanding financial success. Not only will you get the inside track on how to get the most out of a career as a certified golf coach, but you will also learn that establishing and maintaining a quality client list is a crucial aspect of your long-term success.

One unavoidable aspect of helping people to get results is collecting money, that is, if you are unable to sell your service, it is likely that you will be able to continue to give it away? I mean, what are you going to say the next time the golf course owner asks you, "How many golf memberships did you sell last month?" or "How many clients do you have resigning this week?" These are tough issues that nobody wants to write about or face up to. Let's be honest and to the point. **Selling is hard!** It is much easier to just not ask.

The bottom line is, that it is much easier if you have been properly trained on how and when to propose the sale of a golf training package. The anxiety that you are experiencing over asking for money will start to subside after reading this book. I know what you are thinking, "I am a golf coach, not a salesman." I have thought about this a lot and the simple fact of the matter is that you are a counselor, teacher, motivator, coach and sometimes even a psychiatrist, but you are also a salesman. However, not all golf coaches are working for commission, some are actually paid an hourly rate. If you are one of the "fortunate" ones working for a base salary, I am quite certain that it isn't very substantial.

Operationally, your first days working as a golf coach will consist of many long hours of self-education in relation to product knowledge. Sooner or later, you will begin to feel the pressure of the person who is in charge of driving revenue for your particular country club. Whether it's the stress from receiving small paychecks, or the pressure from the person in charge of production in your club, you will feel that it is time to learn how to produce an income from your efforts. Your routine will no doubt start where most golf careers start and you will find yourself taking new clients through a free promotional assessment. Even if your country club does not offer this type of opportunity and you are responsible for creating your own sales opportunities, the fact remains the same. The best way to consistently produce new clients is to offer some sort of orientation or free introductory golf assessment. Success as a golf coach is a derivative of converting these introductory "short term" trials into long-term personal golf coaching clients. If you study the scripts, practicing methods and closing techniques in this book you will have more success than you ever dreamed possible. Soon, the road to financial success as a golf coach will become clear and more enjoyable.

"Confidence is the most important single factor in this game, and no matter how great your natural talent, there is only one way to obtain and sustain it: work." – Jack Nicklaus

As an active golf club operator, I find that I spend a good portion of my time trying to improve the golfing business as a whole. In recent times the golfing industry has been criticized for using questionable business practices. This criticism always seems to center around the shortcomings of the selling process. In my opinion, the focus of this criticism should not be on the selling process. The shortcomings that I have recognized stem from the rapid growth of the golf industry as a whole. This, coupled with a lack of systematic education, as well as the lack of long term employment opportunities are the true issues that plague the golf industry. I have set out not only to increase investor support but also to improve and standardized training. I have tried to develop a process from which golf club owners, managers and employees can systematically develop a long-term healthy plan for investors, members and communities. My systems, like the ones used in my first book *Fitness Memberships and Money* are meant to be internalized so they can be practiced and utilized, although they should merely act as a foundation upon which one can build and improve according to individual needs. I wrote this book with that philosophy in mind. I wrote this book for all the golf coaches that fear going to work at a job they love because they have to sell. I wrote this book to compensate for the certification programs that are misleading young students in regards to the day-to-day life as a golf coach. I wrote this book for all the players that say thank you for changing my game. Thank you for convincing me to make a decision today.

Chapter 2

THE HISTORY OF GOLF

"Hockey is a sport for white men. Basketball is a sport for black men. Golf is a sport for white men dressed like pimps." – Tiger Woods

The Birth of Golf

Golf as we know it today originated from a game played on the eastern coast of Scotland in the Kingdom of Fife during the 15th century. Players would hit a pebble around a natural course of sand dunes, rabbit runs and tracks using a stick or primitive club.

Some historians believe that Kolven from Holland and Chole from Belgium influenced the game. The latter was introduced into Scotland in 1421. However while these games and countless others are stick and ball games, they are missing that vital ingredient that is unique to golf - the hole. Whatever the argument, there can be no dispute that Scotland gave birth to the game we know as golf today.

During the mid-15th century, Scotland was preparing to defend itself against an English invasion. The population's enthusiastic pursuit of golf and soccer to the neglect of military training, caused the Scottish parliament of King James II to ban both sports in 1457. The ban was reaffirmed in 1470 and 1491, although people largely ignored it. Only in 1502 with the Treaty of Glasgow was the ban lifted with King James IV (James 1 of England) himself taking up the sport.

Golf's status and popularity quickly spread throughout the 16th century due to it's royal endorsement. King Charles I popularized the game in England and Mary Queen of Scots, who was French, introduced the game to France while she studied there. Indeed the term *caddie* stems from the name given to her helpers who were the French Military, known in French as cadets.

The premier golf course of the time was Leith near Edinburgh. Indeed King Charles I was on the course when given the news of the Irish rebellion of 1641. Leith was also the scene of the first international golf match in 1682 when the Duke of York and George Patterson playing for Scotland beat two English noblemen.

A Game Becomes a Sport

The Gentlemen Golfers of Leith (1744) was the first club and was formed to promote an annual competition with a silver golf club as the prize. Duncan Forbes drafted the club's rules, which were:

- You must tee your ball within one club's length of the hole.
- Your tee must be on the ground.
- You are not to change the ball which you strike off the tee
- You are not to remove stones, bones or any break club for the sake of playing your ball, except on the fair green, and that only within a club's length of your ball.
- If your ball comes among water, or any watery filth, you are at liberty to take out your ball and bringing it behind the hazard and teeing it, you may play it with any club and allow your adversary a stroke for so getting out your ball.

- If your balls be found anywhere touching one another you are to lift the first ball till you play the last.
- At holeing you are to play your ball honestly for the hole, and not to play upon your adversary's ball, not lying in your way to the hole.
- If you should lose your ball, by its being taken up, or any other way, you are to go back to the spot where you struck last and drop another ball and allow your adversary a stroke for the misfortune.
- No man at holeing his ball is to be allowed to mark his way to the hold with his club or anything else.
- If a ball be stopped by any person, horse or dog, or anything else, the ball so stopped must be played where it lies.
- If you draw your club in order to strike and proceed so far in the stroke as to be bringing down your club; if then your club shall break in any way, it is to be accounted a stroke.
- He who whose ball lies farthest from the hole is obliged to play first.
- Neither trench, ditch or dyke made for the preservation of the links, nor the Scholar's Holes or the soldier's lines shall be accounted a hazard but the ball is to be taken out, teed and played with any iron club.

The club was later renamed the Honorable Company of Edinburgh Golfers with a clubhouse erected in 1768.

The first reference to golf at the historic town of St Andrews was in 1552. The clergy allowed public access to the links a year later. In 1754 the St Andrews Society of Golfers was formed to compete in its own annual competition using Leith's rules. Stroke play was introduced in 1759, and in 1764, the 18-hole course was constructed which has of course become a standard.

The first women's golf club in the world was formed there in 1895. King William honored the club with the title 'Royal & Ancient' in 1834 and the new famous clubhouse was erected in 1854. The Royal and Ancient Golf Club of St Andrews (R&A) became the premier golf club because of its fine course, the publication of rules, its royal patronage and its promotion of the game as a proper sport.

Of course, by this time golfers were using proper clubs and balls. Club heads were made from beech or the wood of fruit trees such as apple. Some club heads for were made from hand-forged iron. Shafts were usually ash or hazel. Balls were made from tightly compressed feathers wrapped in a stitched horse hide sphere. The sport was somewhat exclusive due to the expense of the handcrafted equipment. After 1826, persimmon and hickory were imported from the USA to make club heads and shafts respectively. Today these antiques are highly prized by collectors.

Golf Goes International

"It is nothing new or original to say that golf is played one stroke at a time. But it took me many years to realize it." – Bobby Jones

The British Empire was at its pinnacle during the 19th century. Indeed the phrase 'the sun never sets on the empire' was coined to reflect Britain's world-wide influence. Most of the early golf clubs outside the British Isles and America were formed throughout the Commonwealth.

The first golf club formed outside Scotland was Royal Blackheath (near London) in 1766. However golf is believed to have been played there since 1608. The first golf club outside Britain was the Bangalore, India (1820). Others were the Royal Calcutta (1829), Royal Bombay (1842), Royal Curragh, Ireland (1856), the Pau,

France (1856), the Adelaide (1870), Royal Montreal (1873), Cape Town (1885), St Andrew's of New York (1888) and Royal Hong Kong (1889).

The first golf played in North America that is documented was in Charleston, South Carolina. A Charleston newspaper, the *Gazette*, made mention of scheduled events of the South Carolina Golf Club and referenced its first year as 1786. We can assume that golf was played for several years prior to that date. Being a major east coast port city many of its merchants were Scottish who obviously had access to clubs and balls shipped back to Charleston from abroad.

The Victorian Industrial Revolution brought with it many social and economic changes. The growth of the railways gave birth to the mass tourism industry. For the first time, ordinary people could explore the country as day-trippers or weekend visitors. Golf clubs popped up all over the country and people could enjoy the challenge of playing a different course every weekend.

Due to the expensive nature of the golf equipment which as handcrafted, golf was generally the preserve of the affluent. Once metal club heads and shafts and gutta percha balls (1848) began rolling off the production lines, the average person was able to afford to play golf. Both of these factors directly contributed to the phenomenal growth of golf.

Golf Becomes a Professional Sport

The Prestwick Golf Club was formed in 1851. The precursor to the British Open, the first major national championship, was played there for the first time in 1860 with Willie Park as winner. The legend of Old Tom Morris was born when he won the event in 1862, 1864 and 1867. However his son, Young Tom Morris, was the first great champion winning the event a record four consecutive times from 1869. Other illustrious winners were JH Taylor in 1894 and Harry Vardon in 1896. Together with James Braid, these three men were known as the Great Triumvirate.

Selling Golf

Besides the few sponsored events such as the British Open, most golf professionals made a living from competitions by betting against their opponent. Professionals also earned a living from coaching, ball and club making and caddying.

The growth of golf as an organized competitive sport in the United Kingdom was paralleled abroad in India and the USA. Gate receipts were used as prize money for the first time in 1892 in Cambridge, England. The first international golf tournament was the Amateur Golf Championship of India and the East in 1893.

In 1894, the United States Golf Association (USGA) was established to regulate the game in the United States and Mexico. Besides rules, it managed the handicapping system and conducted research into grass. The US Open and the US Ladies Amateur Open were inaugurated in 1895.

By 1900 there were more than 1000 golf clubs in the USA. Chicago was the first to have 18 holes. Significantly, American golf courses were usually specifically landscaped parklands unlike those in the United Kingdom, which were typically links courses.

The game attracted the attention of the media and business sponsorship, which raised it's profile enormously. In 1897 the first monthly magazine, *Golf*, was published in the USA. The USA became the centre of the professional game due to the proliferation of commercially sponsored competitions. However the prestigious events were still those hosted in the United Kingdom. Interestingly, it was the amateurs rather than professionals, which were exalted by the public.

Golf was confirmed as a global sport when it was made an Olympic sport in 1900.

Birth of the Modern Game

The dawn of the 20th century brought with it several technological innovations. The first was the Haskell one piece rubber cored ball of 1900, which practically guaranteed an extra 20 yards.

Selling Golf

Grooved-faced irons were introduced in 1902. In 1905 William Taylor invented the first dimpled ball. Arthur Knight introduced steel-shafted clubs in 1910 though hickory was widely used for another 25 years. Within the space of a decade, golfers could hit further and more accurately than ever before using equipment which was relatively cheaply mass-produced.

The Professional Golfers Association (PGA) of America was formed in 1916 and initially consisted of a winter calendar. However by 1944 the tour was played throughout the year and consisted of 22 events.

In 1921, the R&A imposed a limit on the size and weight of the golf ball which began a 30 year split between the European and Commonwealth game and the US game (regulated by the USGA). Most of the differences were resolved in 1951, when both parties agreed to a common set of rules, however, the golf ball issue was not settled until 1988. Today golf worldwide is regulated jointly by the R&A and the USGA. They hold a summit every four years where they agree to any alterations to the published official rules of golf.

The rift was accompanied by the introduction of the Ryder Cup matches in 1927. Initially the Europeans were represented by golfers from Britain and Ireland. The Americans with their wealth of talent won every event between 1935 and 1985 with the exception of 1957. Only since 1979, have players outside the British Isles been allowed to play for the European Ryder Cup team and the competition become truly competitive.

Perhaps the greatest player of the pre-war period was the American born Bobby Jones. Amongst his many successes was the original Grand Slam; he won US and British Amateurs and the US and British Opens in 1931. Other luminaries were Sir Henry Cotton who won a third consecutive British Open in 1936 and Walter Hagen who won four British Opens. Hagen was noted for his flamboyant behavior which included hiring a Rolls Royce as a changing room and giving his prize money as winner of the British Open to his caddie.

Great women golfers of the time were Joyce Wethered who won her fifth consecutive English Ladies Championship in 1924 and Glenna Collett Vare who won her sixth US Women's Amateur in 1935.

In 1933, Augusta opened. The first US Masters was played there in 1934 and won by Horton Smith. Gary Player from South Africa broke the American monopoly of the event in 1961. Several British players have won since the 1980s.

When World War II broke out in 1939, competition in England was largely suspended. The War Ministry diverted all rubber and metal resources into the war effort and drafted men of fighting age into the services. The Americans followed suit when they entered the war in 1942.

A Time of Living Memory

The Ladies PGA was formed in 1951 (European version in 1988) and replaced the Women's Professional Golf Association. The first Women's Open was held in 1946 and won by Patty Berg.

Perhaps the greatest lady golfer of the time was Mildred 'Babe' Didrikson Zaharias. She won the US Women's Amateur in 1946, the Women's British Amateur in 1947 and the US Women's Open in 1948, 1950 and 1954. If that wasn't enough, she only took up golf after retiring from an athletics career which included three Olympic gold medals and world records.

After the war, most professionals, with the exception of the great Ben Hogan, chose to compete exclusively in America because of the sizeable prize money on offer. In recognition of this fact, the R&A increased the prize money for the British Open which helped to bring the top players back to Europe.

The 1960s brought with it something special in the guise of Arnold Palmer, Jack Nicklaus and Gary Player - the Modern Triumvirate . They dominated the game into 1970s winning nearly every major event around the world and competing in the prestigious international matches. Nicklaus for example, can claim an unbeaten record of four US Open wins, six US Masters titles and five US PGA Championships.

While the pre-war period might be considered as the age of women's liberation both socially and golf wise, the 1960s brought with it the struggle against bigotry. In 1961, the PGA withdrew its 'whites-only' rule from its constitution. Charlie Sifford became the first black golfer to contest a PGA event and Lee Elder the first to contest the Masters in 1975. However, even in 1990, when the PGA introduced further measures to end racial discrimination, more clubs notably, Cypress Point, withdrew from the Tour. Perhaps Tiger Woods' outstanding victory in the 1997 US Master has finally changed attitudes.

Selling Golf

Golf currently can be considered as the most popular sport in North America and some say the world, with pro golfers earning millions in prize money and sponsorship deals per year. With the rise in fame of Tiger Woods, youngsters have started to pick up the sport, and after many years, golf has finally attained popularity with the mass market and has lost its tag of being a boring old man's game.

Chapter 3

THE DOCTOR

"For me life is continuously being hungry. The meaning of life is not simply to exist, to survive, but to move ahead, to go up, to achieve, to conquer." – Arnold Schwarzenegger

Alvin Stein III had spent much of his life studying to be a doctor. He had devoted his youth to learning about the complicated and diverse systems of the human body. He learned all the technical terms that were important in practicing medicine. Alvin's father and grandfather were both doctors. His father taught him well, ensuring that his son learned everything required of an upcoming successful physician. His father always taught him "that we don't heal books, we heal people." This would become more prevalent in the future.

Alvin was encouraged to become involved in sports and became a good all-around athlete at a young age. He was on the swimming team and the basketball team, earning an award for being the most improved swimmer in his senior year. Alvin received a partial scholarship as a student athlete and he was off to Stanford to begin his college education. He was excited about going to college, especially as he was going to an even more prestigious school than that of his father. He was very enthusiastic about becoming a medical doctor and was excited by the thought of saving a person's life. He was a diligent and hard working student who had joined the swimming team as a requirement of his scholarship, and had gone on to become a letterman with the Varsity Swimming Team.

His college years passed quickly, and he was soon applying for medical school. His participation in athletics helped him mentally and emotionally in areas that left his peers challenged and at times struggling. Understanding the theory was an easy task for some of them, however attempting to utilize and demonstrate their knowledge in a practical manner was often too difficult. Many of the med-students failed to apply this knowledge and information while working on a cadaver. Alvin reflected on what his dad had once said and stated, "My dad was right! We don't heal books; many of the things that we learned in our books are actually very different once you study the anatomy of the human body." As medical school came to an end, Alvin was given the opportunity to complete his internship in Minnesota at the prestigious Mayo Clinic. Things were going well and the time for Alvin to actually commence his medical career was just around the corner!

Alvin moved away from his home in sunny California to complete his studies as an intern. Life was vastly different in Minnesota and he had a difficult time adjusting to the cold weather and the grueling 24-hour shifts. He also had his first feelings of self-doubt in this challenging environment filled with sickness and death. Alvin questioned whether he was capable of achieving his goal of becoming a doctor and called his father weekly for moral support and advice. He informed him of his difficulties and asked him if his internship experience had been similar. Alvin's father offered understanding and encouraged him to be strong, "I completed my internship during a tour in the Vietnam War and it was atrocious. When I came back, being a doctor and running my own clinic was a breeze." He also reminded his son that the internship was designed to be a test. Once the test was over his life of being a doctor would be a breeze as well. Alvin had always wanted to learn the ropes from his dedicated dad. He soon completed his internship and was ready to start working in his father's busy clinic.

Alvin was doing well and business was thriving. However, soon after, a distressing problem arose. The insurance companies were changing their policies, leaving older patients with insufficient coverage for adequate health care. Matters worsened when an elderly patient that Alvin had been treating passed away leaving his widow with medical bills and rejected insurance. This was starting to put serious pressure on the business and on Alvin's life. He began dreading work and the day soon came when he had to tell his father that was going to leave the medical field.

His father said, "Son, I have been waiting for this day to come. I had hoped it wouldn't, but the day is here and I have something special for you. Your Grandfather said this was an area of weakness in his profession. You see, your Grandfather was a genuine-and good hearted man and back in those days people were poor. They would die because they couldn't afford to pay the doctor. Your grandfather gave away so much free medical care that he himself went bankrupt. This book was given to your grandfather and it was an instrumental part of your Grandfather's ability to recover from financial ruin. It was given to your grandfather from a teacher at Harvard. The book was never published and it was really made up from secret techniques used by Harvard doctors who had run very successful clinics. The book mainly focused on a different side of being a doctor. The cover of the book had only two words on it simply reading, 'Selling Medicine.' The book was not only given to your grandfather but it was also given to another doctor who was in your same situation. It was given to a doctor who had an incredible talent to cure the sick and was ready to give up. This book has a reputation for being the savior of many generations of doctors."

As Alvin's father pulled the book from an old dusty box, he explained that he searched high and low to find the book because he knew that it had meant so much to his father. "I also knew that someday it just might come in handy. Now my son, I give the book to you. May you let the age-old words encompass the art of being a master of our trade. We must thank the hard-won work of those who have come before us, while also challenging and emulating their success in all areas." As Alvin opened the book, he noticed the penciled in writing. "My son this is a true story and it is to remind you that every case is as different in nature as the ailment from which it has come, some times the heart is the only medicine needed."

(I am not talking about the patients, this book is to heal the Doctor!)

Selling Golf

"A Red Cross soldier"

One day, a Red Cross soldier, who was selling everything in his bag from door to door to pay his way back over the border, found he had only one thin dime left. You see his plane had crash-landed during a peace mission, and he was very hungry.

He decided he would ask for a meal at the next house. However, he lost his nerve when a lovely young woman opened the door. Instead of a meal, he asked for a drink of water.

She thought he looked hungry, so she brought him a large bowl of soup. He ate it slowly, and then asked, "How much do I owe you?"

You don't owe me anything," she replied. "Mother has taught us never to accept pay for a kindness." He said, "Then I thank you from my heart."

As Alvin Stein left that house, he not only felt stronger physically, but his faith in man was stronger. He had been ready to give up and quit. Many years later, that same young woman became critically ill.

The local doctors were baffled. They finally sent her to the big city, where they called in specialists to study her rare disease. Dr. Alvin Stein was called in for the consultation. When he heard the name of the town she came from, a strange light filled his eyes. Immediately, he rose and went down the hall to her room.

Dressed in his doctor's gown, he went in to see her. He recognized her at once. He went back to the consultation room and was determined to do his best to save her life. From that day, he gave special attention to her case. After a long struggle, the battle was won.

Dr. Stein requested the business office to pass the final bill to him for approval. He looked at it, and then wrote something on the edge and the bill was sent to her room. She feared to open it, for she was sure it would take the rest of her life to pay this bill.

Finally she looked, and something caught her attention on the side of the bill. She then read these words...

"Paid in full with one bowl of soup"

(Signed) Dr. Alvin Stein.

Tears of joy flooded her eyes as her happy heart prayed: "Thank You, God, that your love has spread broad through human hearts and hands."

You should remember this story my son! This book was given to me by a friend to help me cope with my own personal fear of dealing with the business side of being a doctor. You must trust your heart and remember not every case is the same.

Your father, Alvin Stein the first

This was written in pencil by his own hand in the front of your Grandfathers book!

"Dad, are you saying that he gave this book to you?" "You were the doctor that was ready to give up, and Grandpa gave the book to you?" "WHAT IS THE BOOK REALLY ABOUT?" "It will teach you how to ask for money and make a living as a doctor!"

"My son, there are three different kinds of doctors in this world; the first are the ones that own clinics, they are good businessmen and they make the most money. The second are the doctors that work for the hospitals, they are the ones that don't like dealing with the business side so they let the hospitals deal with most of it, but they still get some of the patients coming back to them. The third is the doctor like the ones that do research and teach at schools, they hate the business side so much that they didn't even talk about it for the entire 12 years that they spent at medical school. The business end of being a doctor brings out their worst fears and most of them were never willing to face those fears head on by taking up the challenge. Son, in all jobs there will be some parts that you may not like!"

"SOME PEOPLE WILL FOLD UP TENT AND QUIT, THE STEINS FOCUS!"

Chapter 4

HOW THE SYSTEM WORKS

The system operates through constant repetition. It relies on systematic improvement of skills through practice. The system works with proven techniques to be used and referenced. Different areas of your arsenal must be used over and over in "real life" (role playing) situations until they are perfected. The system must be used and not merely read. When teaching systems, I get my staff to practice role-playing situations as opposed to me standing up and talking to them. This way I can be certain that they have learned the material, that they know how to use the scripts and that they are ready to deal with clients. I then make them present in front of a large group or the staff. If they can perform in front of the entire sales team, they can present it to a player or several potential clients.

"If you are a manager and you want to know the key to success? Inspect everything you expect!"

I also make the staff accountable to have the scripts memorized by a certain date. If they do not have them memorized, then I make them present it to me every day until they do. Remember, the accountability factor is the key to managing the golf club and yourself simultaneously. Nothing will be accomplished without accountability. If you are a self-starter this may be easy for you. If you are not, this task may take a little more time. You have to turn any system that you use in the golf club into a habit. Once something is a habit, it becomes easier, enabling you to enjoy it more. The goals you set for yourself must be as important as the ones you set for your clients. You must approach them in the same manner: one step at a time.

When small business golf clubs transformed into big businesses, investors desired standardized systems. This is when I came into the picture. I worked for one of the largest golf clubs in California. We had just reached a significant milestone and we had received a large injection of cash to expand our company even further. Golf lessons had just become something that was offered to our members and I had the unique opportunity to work in a club that had been allocated for the pilot program.

A pilot program is where you take a new system and you test it and try it in one particular location. Once you have taken a core system and developed it into something that works, you then work out the bugs and problems and finally you implement your system into the rest of the organization. Programs like these are developed with very careful planning and implemented under the watchful supervision of company management. The teams chosen for this difficult task were handpicked to deliver optimum results. As the system for selling golf lessons was developed, I had the opportunity to work as a training package counselor and was able to help bring this incredible new program to the front lines.

We were a fantastic group of highly motivated individuals. We drank the potion and bought into the company systems, 110%. We believed that we were part of something that was going to change the industry and that we could make a difference in the lives of our golf members. The system that we created took several months and underwent many transformations before it became the product that most golf clubs use today. Thousands of people have benefited from the results and the systems that were created during this pilot program. It is amazing the kind of energy you can create from a group of individuals that believe and work toward achieving a common goal. I believe that my ability to build successful teams has come from my ability to duplicate this atmosphere in all the clubs that I operate.

Having one or two extraordinarily talented individuals can never compare with having a group of untalented, hardworking, system-believing people focused on one common success story. I feel that of all the golf lesson systems that I have seen in the 35 clubs that I have managed, this system has topped them all!

> *"If you are a new Golf Coach, the first thing you must do is memorize the sale presentation scripts word for word."*

Soon after this program was developed, there was another large acquisition in California. The two largest golf clubs merged and tried to combine their systems, leaving behind some of the secrets that built these wonderful organizations. I have had the privilege to see both systems at work in golf courses all over the world. Chicago to Nevada, California to China! The words and systems used in this book will unmistakably without a doubt improve your ability to sell Golf.

Chapter 5

GOLF COACH PLANNER

Training materials should be kept in the front of your planner and should be referenced as often as possible or whenever needed. As discussed in Chapter 4, I prefer my coaches to memorize various scripts for different situations. Memorizing these scripts is the first thing a new golf coach should do. If you are unable to memorize the ten or so pages of script, you should do nothing else until you perfect that area of your arsenal. If you are not able to perform an effective trial training package appointment, and if you do not know how to present golf or how to set up a take over (TO), then you should practice in these areas before taking any players. Once these scripts are memorized, such as the introduction, then these training materials will be used as a reference and training tool. It sounds like a lot of work, but believe me it makes the job easier and more profitable.

Once a month you should train in each area of the book. If you do this, your sales skills will remain sharp and you will have the ability to learn and grow. Remember, the golf industry is a rapidly growing business and change is essential for continued growth and improvement. If certain areas of the training process are not working or you are not improving, then you, as a professional, have to improve the training information you are using.

"If you fail to plan, you plan to fail"

To-Do List

I found that the personal to-do list is a simple and effective tool that has been used for years by everyone from housewives to the President of the United States. It is a simple concept. When you think of something that is important, write it down! This will put it on your priority list, limiting mistakes and leaving your mind free to think of other things. You can cross off each task as you accomplish it and remaining items can be circled and transferred to the next day's to-do list. This can be an effective habit. I find that people who use this simple tool are more efficient, make fewer mistakes, and get more accomplished. Although this is your business planner, personal matters can still be taken care of at work. It is okay to list personal matters on your to-do list.

Goals and Projections

Goals and projections should be updated daily. This is the most functional way of learning how your production can influence your numbers. As the old saying goes, "the numbers do not lie." This is especially true in our business. The numbers tell us what we are doing right and what we are doing wrong. They are our guides to success. They will show you what happens when you have a bad day, and they will show you what happens when you have a good day. Most importantly, they will show you what happens when you are not set up for that day.

My definition of a successful person is a person that can set goals and then achieve those goals.

What happens to your paycheck when you hit your goals? I bet you can answer that question for yourself. Having an organized "Goals and Projections" section in your planner will show you what you have to do daily; it gives you the ability to control your numbers more consistently and will offer you a daily affirmation of your goals. I prefer to track every area of sales separately. Within each area, I have five steps:

Gross Sales: goal, last day worked, month to date, projection and percentage

EFT: goal, last day worked, month to date, projection and percentage

Golf: goal, last day worked, month to date, projection and percentage

Supplements: goal, last day worked, month to date, projection and percentage

Retail: goal, last day worked, month to date, projection and percentage

Other goals: last day worked, month to date, projection and percentage

If kept updated consistently and correctly, these areas will keep us more organized and help increase our sales. We begin by setting goals and then use our materials to project our progress as we go along. Each month you should set goals based on the previous month's performance. Like most successful salespeople, your sales goal should increase each month, as your ability to hit these goals increases. As you hone your sales skills, your comfort level and confidence increase, enabling you to achieve higher goals. I personally never set goals that are too easy to achieve. At the same time, I never set goals that are impossible to achieve. You want the goal to be lofty enough to motivate you but not so high that you cannot achieve it.

The goal should be in line with what you want your paycheck to be. If you set a goal that is $200,000 in sales and your commission is 10 percent, you will earn $20,000 commission before taxes; therefore, you cannot expect to bring home a $30,000 paycheck! The first goal that should be set is what you want your income to be. Based on that, you can calculate how much you need to sell. You now have your goal.

For Example:

Your desired income is $50,000	50,000
Your commission from each sale is 10%	x10
You must sell	$500,000

Selling Golf

Being able to meet your goals will make you a highly effective golf coach and you will be able to control your financial destiny. The sky is the limit! The last day worked column is what you sold the last day in each area. The month to date column is a running total; it represents the updated total amount you have sold up to that date for the month. The projection column is the month to date divided by the days gone by, times the total days in the month. The percentage column is your projection divided by your goal.

For example for Projection:

> month to date   divided by days gone by.
>
> x
>
> Total days in the month. = Projection

It is the second day of a 30-day month. Yesterday you sold $2,000 in gross sales. Your month to date is $2,000. One day has gone by, and so you divide 2000 by 1, times 30 days in the month. It means that the total amount you are projecting is $60,000. Divide that by your goal of $70,000. You are at 86 percent of your goal.

For example:

$$\frac{2{,}000 \times 30}{1} = 60{,}000 = 86\%$$
$$70{,}000$$

You now have 29 days left in the month to reach your goal. Since you sold $2,000 on the first day of the month, you now have only $68,000 left to reach your goal. In order to find your daily goal you must subtract your month to date from your goal, and divide by how many days are left in the month. The numbers show that you must sell an average of $2,344 per day for the rest of the month to achieve 100 percent of your original goal.

For example:

$$\begin{array}{r} 70{,}000 \\ -\ 2{,}000 \\ \hline 68{,}000 \end{array} \qquad \frac{68{,}000}{29} = \$2{,}344$$

Updating your statistics is something that should be done every day. You should make this a strict habit and it should be the first thing you do every morning after you walk through the club. The numbers, good or bad, will show you the areas that you have to focus on for that day. They also show the areas that you are doing well in and the areas that need improvement.

Finally, your daily appointment sheets will have areas for all important appointment information. Each day's sheet will have sections for logging the time of the appointment, for confirmation, the person's name, their work and home telephone number, a note about the appointment, and finally, the outcome.

Appointments

The **time** section stands for what time you are scheduling the appointment. You write the individual's information next to the time they are expected to arrive for their appointment. You should highlight certain areas of the day to be filled in by the front desk and/or the sales staff to ensure that your appointment book is filled with high quality orientations. The **confirmation** box will allow you to make a note if the appointment has been confirmed. In addition one should check the book regularly to see if any new appointments have been scheduled. It is also advisable to call and reconfirm prior to an appointment to save you from being inconvenienced, for example driving into work only to have to leave again because your appointment failed to show. Finally, ensure that all of your clients are able to contact you at anytime with last minute cancellations. (Please see chapter 30, page 152, Confirming appointments and cancellations.)

Selling Golf

Monthly Success Plan

(Name)_____   (Month)_____

GOAL

Gross_____ EFT_____ PT_____ Other_____

**I will complete the steps below and hit my
personal goals by the end of this month.**

1、 _____
   _____

2、 _____
   _____

3、 _____
   _____

4、 _____
   _____

5、 _____
   _____

6、 _____
   _____

(Signature)_____   (Date)_____
(Manager)_____   (Date)_____

If you want to be better than 75% of people, show up to work on time.

If you want to be better than 80% of people, show up to work on time dressed in uniform.

If you want to be better than 90% of people, show up to work on time, dressed in uniform with a plan.

Selling Golf

This is your monthly plan, live by it! Learn to adjust it based on your performance, you can accomplish anything in life if you know how to set a plan and work your plan.

MONTHLY CALENDAR

SUNDAY	MONDAY	TUESDAY	WEDNESDAY	THURSDAY	FRIDAY	SATURDAY
SUNDAY	MONDAY	TUESDAY	WEDNESDAY	THURSDAY	FRIDAY	SATURDAY
SUNDAY	MONDAY	TUESDAY	WEDNESDAY	THURSDAY	FRIDAY	SATURDAY
SUNDAY	MONDAY	TUESDAY	WEDNESDAY	THURSDAY	FRIDAY	SATURDAY
SUNDAY	MONDAY	TUESDAY	WEDNESDAY	THURSDAY	FRIDAY	SATURDAY
SUNDAY	MONDAY	TUESDAY	WEDNESDAY	THURSDAY	FRIDAY	SATURDAY

Selling Golf

TODAY'S GUEST APPOINTMENTS

TIME	SOURCE	CONF	NAME	PHONE #	RESULTS	TIME	SOURCE	CONF	NAME	PHONE #	RESULT
8AM						3PM					
:30						:30					
9AM						4PM					
:30						:30					
10AM						5PM					
:30						:30					
11AM						6PM					
:30						:30					
12PM						7PM					
:30						:30					
1PM						8PM					
:30						:30					
2PM						9PM					
:30						:30					

All missed guests should be given passes and have appointment on closeout

Missed Guest without Pass: Blue
MIssed Guest with Pass: Yellow
Enrolled Guest: Green
DI & NI: Orange

Selling Golf

Golf Coach Tracking Sheet

Coach Name: Package Purchase Date:

Client Name: Total Sessions:

Client Phone No.:

	Client's Name	Date of Session	Time of Session	Signature
1				
2				
3				
4				
5				
6				
7				
8				
9				
10				
11				
12				
13				
14				
15				
16				

Selling Golf

Meeting Notes

<u>All</u> notes taken at our club for any reason should be put in the notes section of your planner, if it is written anywhere else, it will get lost.

Selling Golf

Chapter 6

THE LANGUAGE OF SALES

Rejection Words	**Acceptable Substitutes**
Contract	Golf training agreement, Agreement, Paperwork, Form
Cost or Price	Investment or Amount
Down Payment	Initial Investment, Initial Amount, One-time Investment
Monthly Payment	Monthly Investment or Monthly Amount
Sell or Sold	Get involved or Get started
Deal	Package or Opportunity
Pay For	Take care of
Sign	Authorize, Approve, Endorse, OK it
Crowded	Popular, Exciting, Active Environment
Salesperson	Coach, Golf Coach
Dollars	Omit this word altogether—the only possible exception is when the player is comparison shopping, and your club is a better value because it will save him or her so many dollars per session or package
Commission	Fee for service
Objection	Concern
If	When
Cheap	Affordable
Diet	Nutritional Program, Food Intake
Pitch, Spiel.	Presentation
High Pressure	Enthusiasm, Concern
Prizewinner, "up" here	Player, Client
On a free pass or walk-in Sign up, join.	Get involved, Get started

"Victorious warriors win first and then go to war, while defeated warriors go to war first and then seek to win." --Suntzu

It is important to know that certain words can create an emotional response from your prospective golf clients. It is important to practice and use only the words that are going to work in your favor.

For Example

"Mom I'm going to the golf club to get a personal coaching package." The mother responds, *"Make sure you don't sign anything without reading it first and make sure you don't get involved in any contracts!"*

People remember these little things. I don't know why but they just seem to pop up when we use certain words. So practice using the right words and your job will be a lot easier, just like second nature.

Chapter 7

HOW TO SPEAK TO A GUEST

Building instant rapport can come from something as simple as addressing a person by their first name.

A true sales professional and golf coach understands the basic fundamentals when it comes to speaking to a potential client. Rapport and comfort levels with a client can be created or destroyed almost immediately.

It may sound redundant, but make certain to do the following:

1. Smile, use a firm handshake and maintain eye contact.
2. A proper greeting and introduction is essential. Be sure to introduce yourself and use the client's name.
3. Build rapport by asking many questions. A proper needs analysis can be the key to making the sale. Do not give up too much information before you truly understand your potential client's intentions. (Use your country club's orientation card and perform a proper needs analysis.)
4. Be kind and courteous at all times and be sure to let your client do most of the talking. *(You have two ears and one mouth for a reason!)*
5. It is important to remain indirect when attempting to close the sale. You must develop the ability to maintain good rapport through five closing attempts. (This will only happen if you use the steps outlined in Chapter 18, How to Overcome Objections.)

Sales language

Only seven percent of all communication is verbal, which is a fact that many people find hard to believe. Ninety three percent of our communication has nothing to do with the words that you produce, but more to do with the non-verbal communication that we use. Non-verbal communication consists of tone of voice, eye contact, facial expressions, and proximity to another person. All of these factors come into play when you're communicating with another individual. A sales person or golf coach's inability to endear this concept can very easily limit their revenue production and personal income levels. Let's look at this scenario:

One coach presents a personal training package to a prospective client, but they do not purchase it. Another coach steps in and performs a full transference of emotions into that prospective client and sells them a package while using the exact same words that the first coach used. The reason why this happens is that you may be talking to your client, but you are not really *communicating* with them. A full transference of emotions is making your prospect feel what you are feeling, the passion for fitness and the need for proper education through a Golf coach!

There are different ways to communicate the same words, each providing a different meaning to the receiver. You can look at someone and smile, then laugh and call him or her a name. You can also scream in someone's face and call him or her a name. These are two vastly different forms of communication with totally different meanings. They will also achieve two totally different results. You have to be aware of how and what you are communicating. You must help your prospect to understand that you truly care and want to help them attain their personal goals. These are techniques that come naturally to some people and are often difficult to teach. It takes a lot of trial and error. Some people pick up the knack of communicating, or they may have learned naturally through their parents or other experiences. The bottom-line is that it is very important to pin point the communication style of your player.

The true meaning of sales is the transference of emotions. Your prospect needs to truly feel and believe in what you are saying. You will come to the point where you learn how to manipulate through communication. This happens once you have memorized the scripts, inserted your personality into them, and effectively learned how to "mirror" your prospect. These certain forms of communication are less verbal than you may think. The first step in learning the sales process is verbal communication: saying the right words, asking the right questions, getting the person to agree by "using tie downs," all the things that can come across the desk verbally.

The T.O. process will enable you to watch your manager and listen to other salespeople who may be better than or more experienced than you. You will begin to learn that there are other areas of communication such as the non-verbal. This form of communication creates the certain energy that flows across the desk and can't be heard. Have you ever shown a player the prices and observed their face turning red? No doubt you start to sense the friction at the table even though they haven't said a word. You can clearly see the non-verbal communication coming across the table, the red face and the moving in the seat. You can feel all of the emotions that your player is projecting. That flow of energy coming across the desk is what I am talking about. A professional knows how to harness and control that energy and use it to close more packages.

"Your first week as salesperson, you should try a game I invented. For one week answer every question asked with a question. This will help you understand the fundamentals of sales!"

Why do you get up from a sales presentation? What does it accomplish? It clears the air of all the emotions that were flowing back and forth between you and the player, and enables them to relax. One of your goals is to comfort your client, which can be achieved by helping them to loosen up and feel good about making a purchase. They can't do that if they feel the friction across the desk. There is no denying that people project energy and you should make sure that you are aware of this. Study this and know that it can hold you back from making sales.

You can say all the right things to a player and everything may seem to be going well, but there is still something missing. What is it? They feel uncomfortable and uneasy about buying a package from *you*. You said all the right things and were nice to the person, but deep down inside the potential client felt that you weren't being honest or they felt that something just wasn't right. The greeting and introduction is an overlooked but vital aspect of our business. Many club managers and golf coaches neglect to devise a uniform greeting strategy when faced with a prospective member.

Greeting and Introduction

This is an area that, when focused on correctly, will improve the relationship with the client, decrease tension and ultimately lead to an increase of sales. There are many different ways of doing this but remember that, "you never get a second chance to make a first impression." See the following script as an example of the method that I prefer to use in this situation.

"How are you?" (Wait for response)

"My name is John, and what is your name?" (Wait for response)

"Mr. Soon to be client, what I would like to do is take a moment of your time to find out exactly what it is you are looking to accomplish? Then I will ask you a couple of questions in regard to your current golf skill level and goals on the course. Finally, when we are finished, I will take you through basic one on one price options. Sound fair?" (Wait for response)

"Great."

Since I believe in a consistent system approach, I feel it is important to avoid making the introduction too complicated. Many coaches will not use a system approach for fear it will limit their personality and many employers fear that they may not be able to successfully teach it to new employees. They view it as more of a burden than it is worth, avoiding the implementation of a standard introduction and presentation, which can, in effect, be detrimental to sales.

Building Rapport

In order to consistently produce sales of any type, one must build rapport with a prospective client. Building good rapport allows you to build a comfort zone and a trust level between yourself and the prospect. If there is no trust, there is no sale.

You must attempt to think as they would think and you must be patient and mindful of their questions and concerns. People rarely trust those they do not like or feel comfortable with. Being humble and kind in all situations will help to earn this trust.

Take a moment to think of the people you surround yourself with. I am going to guess that you probably trust and like the people that you call "friends". The most successful sales people in this business build mini-relationships with the majority of their prospects. Having good rapport means that you communicate well with another person, you are friendly, and you trust one another. If you think of each prospect as a potential friend, you will immediately find yourself more comfortable when speaking with them. The easiest way to build a strong rapport with your prospect is by uncovering possible common interests that you may have. It is easy for a person to say "no" to a person they do not like, or a person they have nothing in common with.

Remember the **K-I-S-S** rule. It means **Keep It Simple Stupid!** Even though you want to build rapport and find common interests, you want to do this in a simple, comfortable fashion. Be careful not to offer too much information about yourself before discovering what their interests are. Ask your prospect questions and find common interests based on their answers. Giving up too much information about yourself before you know the interests of your client can cause problems that are hard to overcome.

For example, John is attempting to sell a one on one package to Tom. Tom explains that he is a huge football fan, he lives in the Bay Area, and football is his life. John replies that the Bay Area is a beautiful place, and he loves San Francisco. "Go 49ers!" Tom explains that he lives in Oakland, and he is a Raiders fan!

In this situation, the salesperson did not find out the proper information before speaking. The salesperson was too quick with his response and did not pre-qualify. Therefore, since Tom's life is football, now opposite interests have been established and John's sale is now increasingly more difficult.

The salesperson/prospect relationship is one of give and take. You will find yourself in situations where you share no common interests with a prospect. In fact, you are not going to care in the least about some of their interests and quite often you will find yourself disagreeing with their opinions. These are the times when you must remember that you are a professional, not a fan, and you are the one who must stay in control. Always try to keep a smile on your face and keep after *your* goal.

Mirroring and Matching

Along with memorizing your scripts, you must learn to "mirror" your prospects. Mirroring allows one to build rapport by utilizing the same voice tones, facial expressions, and body language as the person they are engaging. We will always feel more comfortable with someone that we feel parity with. The most successful sales people in the world not only find common bonds verbally, but do so physically as well. This is a very vital and overlooked aspect of being a golf coach and a salesperson.

You **must** find common ground with your potential client as this can be the difference between gaining a new client and losing one. When used properly, mirroring means having the ability to change the way you act, talk, and the speed in which you react or walk in accordance with the prospective client. This is not something that I can outline for you. It is not something that is easy to teach. It is an effective tool that, when mastered, can make an unbelievable impact on your sales numbers and your income.

For Example:

If the prospect is shy, you cannot be aggressive. If you have a prospect that walks slowly, you cannot walk fast. If your prospect talks quietly, you need to talk quietly. If your prospect leans back and crosses their legs during your sales presentation, you need to do so as well. Get the picture?

This area of your arsenal can go much deeper. You have to be like a chameleon, a lizard that has the ability to change its color and shape to meet its surroundings.

Chapter 8

THE GOLF ORIENTATION TRIAL

"I never hit a shot, not even in practice, without having a very sharp, in-focus picture of it in my head. First I see the ball where I want it to finish, nice and white and sitting up high on the bright green grasss. Then the scene quickly changes, and I see the ball going there: its path, trajectory, and shape, even its behavior on landing. Then there is a sort of fade-out, and the next scene shows me making the kind of swing that will turn the previous images into reality" – Jack Nicklaus

The golf orientation trial, or complimentary pro session, has become a very important aspect of the golf training package sales process. As the golf training sales process began to evolve, we found that the most difficult obstacle to overcome was getting the golf coaches to go out on to the range and take a player through a complimentary clinic. It has proven to be difficult to get coaches to approach players and offer their services. We felt that the key to a successful golf club operation must lie in getting our client results. We found that most of the players that dropped out of the private pro lessons were the ones that didn't see any improvement within the first 6 weeks.

As a remedy to these two problems, we developed a program that would benefit coaches and players alike. It would give the coaches an opportunity to offer their services as well as giving every single member an opportunity to work with a coach possessing the knowledge to set a successful program in motion. This program could show the benefits and the value of the personal coaching program. We truly felt that the success of the golf club would depend on producing quality opportunities for the coaches.

We also felt that every individual who joined the country club should get a chance to experience some golfing education. At that time, we made the decision that every person, whether they joined on a training package or were given a free pass to the club, would receive three sessions with a golf coach. At the end of the third session, they would be brought to the table and given a presentation or talk about how their trial training sessions went. We would also find out what equipment or clubs they needed, and if they were interested in continuing with personal coaching.

Keep Them Coming

In order to be a successful coach you must keep a consistent influx of new clients coming your way. There are several ways of doing this. One way is to be able to work the field. The other way is to produce a great line of quality buddy referrals. The only problem with this is that they require a natural sales ability. We have found that many coaches were unable to use this system consistently. The best coaches in our business were the ones that had the ability to pick and choose clients based on consistent re-signing of clients, continued trial sign ups, and a dedication toward reaching their goals. If you maintain a consistent approach towards creating daily orientation you will be booked with quality golf clients. The over sold clients can easily be passed down to other pros on the golf course that have fewer clients or may just be starting out. Pick and choose the clients you work well with. Build a relationship with other golf coaches, and allocate a system to send over bookings to these newer or less fortunate team members. Remember the more quality clients you train and maintain, the more you can charge for your service.

In review, every member who joined the club was offered three free forty minute coaching sessions to orientate the members to the club. The original program consisted of a three step process.

#1 a questionnaire and a golf handicap assessment followed by a short test. #2 session consisted of a basic driving introduction on the range. #3 session consisted of basic putting practice on the greens and a brief presentation of the benefits of other training package services and personal coaching.

The Orientation Card

I felt that the early orientation program worked well and produced great numbers. The program that I now recommend for best results has come from a modified system that has been tested, tried and improved. Your orientation cards or questionnaires will vary from club to club depending on your particular demographic. It is important to understand that your particular company has put a lot of time and effort into creating this service to the players. I believe that if you have been properly trained and you do a quality orientation, you will find that in most cases your club has created substantial value using their orientation card. Looking at the orientation program from an ownership stand point, most companies have determined that this program has substantial cost involved and many of the large golf clubs have shortened this program to meet financial obligations. Whether your company offers one complimentary session or ongoing sessions, the fact remains the same. Offering free golf lessons and using your company's standardized goal sheet will improve your selling ability.

Here are some pointers:

- Scheduling quality orientations and making sure that you have several each and everyday will improve your business.
- Book orientations for times that you have openings in your schedule. Most likely your potential clients will book their orientation at the same time they are interested in receiving the personal coaching sessions

- It is important to use the communication skills outlined in Chapter 7 and to build rapport with your potential client. Even if the player is not interested in ongoing sessions, they are still very important to the club and your first impression may be a lasting one.

- It is important to be informative but equally important to ask questions, make notes and pay close attention to the education level of your potential client. Using technical information may overwhelm or invoke fear.

- It is important to spend some time on the written part of the interview but it is also equally important to spend time building rapport and not focusing so much on the technical and the written parts of the interview. Spending more time understanding the person can be more important than their golf handicap.

- Normally, as a rule of thumb, we do not present personal coaching on the first session. In some cases, your potential client may show an interest in personal coaching sessions during your first interview. If this were the case, I would recommend doing a full presentation on the one-on-one sessions available.

- Depending on which presentation you like best, I would recommend learning it word for word until you are so comfortable that you can add your own personality and style. Once you have done this, your presentation should sound smooth and should not sound memorized.

Selling Golf

Chapter 9

THE GOLF ORENTATION CARD

Date:_____   G.O.1   G.O.2
Guest Name:_____   _____ _____
Coach:_____

Name:_____ Date of birth:_____Age:_____
Address: _____
Phone:(H)_____(O)_____(HP)_____
E-mail:_____ Occupation:_____
Emergency Contact:_____

Health Screening

Have you had or ever experienced:

❏ Dizziness or fainting?   ❏ Any pain or injury to the joints

❏ Any heart condition   ❏ Pregnant or given birth in the past 1 year

❏ High(low)Blood pressure   ❏ Any major surgery

❏ Stroke   ❏ Any other medical conditions that we

❏ Diabetes   should be aware of?

I am aware that physical exercise can subject me to serious injury and that if I engage in physical activity or use any Number One Golf Club facility or participate in any Number One Golf Club sponsored event I do so entirely at my own risk. I release Number One Golf Club and its directors, officers, and agents from any liability to me or damage or loss to any of my personal property in connection with my use of Number One Golf Club facilities or equipment or my participation in Number One Golf Club sponsored activities. I understand that I am giving up legal rights that I might otherwise have and that this release includes without limitation, damages I may suffer as a result of (1) my use of any equipment, product or Number One Golf Club facility, (ii) the malfunctioning of any Number One Golf Club equipment, (iii) any Number One Golf Club instruction or supervision, and (iv) slipping, falling, or otherwise injuring myself in any manner while on the Number One Golf Club premises, including sidewalks and parking.

Client Signature:_____Date:_____

Personal Goals

Please check on the goals you want to achieve in embarking on golf training:

❑ Improve grip   ❑ Improve focus

❑ Improve on a sport specific performance   ❑ Improve swing techniques

❑ Improve stance   ❑ Improve putting

❑ improve techniques   ❑ How to gain those extra yards in your drive

❑ Increase strength   ❑ Social

On the scale of 1-5, how would you rate your current golf handicap?
(1, 2, 3, 4, 5)
Can you give a brief description of your problem with your golf game?
_____

When was the last time that you felt that played the perfect game of golf?
_____

Selling Golf

Please list a brief description of an average game of golf in the last two months. Please include driving range time and putting sessions.
_____

What is the most convenient time for golf practice, morning, afternoon or evening?
_____

What is your current work or school schedule?
_____

How much time would you be allocating towards accomplishing your desired golf handicap?
_____

Chapter 10

MY ONE ON ONE GOLF PRESENTATION

"Expose yourself to various conditions and learn." – Bruce Lee

This is the point where I am given the opportunity to reveal the presentation that really changed the face of golf. For the majority of the coaches back in the days when these pilot programs were being developed, selling their service was the last thing on their mind. The golf coach was just a guy or girl out on the course that helped give some good pointers and maybe once in awhile, if you were lucky or good looking, you would get some rich old person to pay money to have you teach them how to putt. Most of the coaches honestly believed that the service they provided was reserved only for a certain class! If I was to stereo-type, the average young, new golf coach did not believe in their own self worth and to most young coaches 50 dollars for 1 hour of their coaching services was just an unheard of amount of money. So, we decided to make it our goal to find out where the shortcomings were in the golfing area.

Once we pinpointed what the shortcomings actually were, we set our goal and then we developed a plan of how we would overcome each of our obstacles. It may sound rather scientific but this was a business plan and we confronted it accordingly. We realized that the golf coaching department could be one of the fastest growing revenue centers in our country clubs. We believed that we could set ourselves apart by offering the most successful program to our players. We truly believed that we could create a way of life that generated results. If we could teach our members that by using private coaching sessions to develop good effective habits people from all walks of life would be able to enjoy the benefits of golf. A large percentage of top athletes, successful movie actors, and even executives have worked with professional coaches to achieve maximum results.

We knew what the major key to our business was, always stay focused and remember that the main obstacle would be getting results. It was also important that we understand a successful system for learning how to sell golf. We believed that the first step in selling golf was to get potential clients in front of a coach so that they would understand what it is that the coaches do. The second step is that you must understand the benefits of the personal coaching program. The third step is to develop a presentation that builds the value of this extremely precious program. The fourth step is presenting the different price options and the fifth step is getting the commitment and closing the sale.

Step One: Understanding What It Is the Coaches Do

We believed that the coaches needed a benefits building program that would be so powerful that no closing was necessary, the following is what was created.

The coaches do:

goal setting for the player, setting achievable goals within a specific time frame and putting everything down on paper. This ensures that the member can track their improvement. The coaches also focus on other important areas such as those outlined below.

Golf Swing, proper ways of swinging the club to enhance distance

Accountability, ensuring that the players show up to their scheduled appointments.

Consistency, making sure that the player is playing on a consistent basis, about 3 to 4 times per week.

Motivation, is needed to consistently hit your goals and ensure that you get the most out of every single golf lesson.

Proper grip, to avoid injuries and to ensure the optimal benefit to the player.

Program Design, individualizing the program to achieve long-term results and a lifetime education of golf. Tie downs were added at the end of each step to gain minor agreement.

Step Two: The Benefits of Golf Coaching

The benefits of golf are endless, but I will single out a few: a better game, more consistant handicaps through practice; an education that will stay with you for the duration of your life; better player self-esteem; a positive impact on your personal relationships; better performance at work; more energy; health; and lower stress levels. This is just a portion of the benefits. The possibilities are endless.

Step Three: The Presentation of Benefits

I personally recommend that you come up with a script that will build up the benefits and add value to your presentation. I used a script developed by one of the top golf coach in our company at the time. Your script may resemble a script like this one (refer to chapter 7, page 38) or the one I recommended previously for the greeting and introduction. I worked with an outstanding golf coach who lent his script to all the salespeople to help them increase personal coaching sales. It was three pages long and it took me a month to memorize, but it worked great. The first month I used the presentation my sales went through the roof and I sold $9,000 in personal coaching. It focuses on building the benefits of the training program and helps the player to understand exactly what they are paying $50 an hour for.

Remember, you cannot show a person in one hour precisely what it is the golf coach is going to help them accomplish. Therefore, you have to paint a picture in the persons mind of the benefits they are going to receive from this service. If the benefits outweigh the loss, your member will be willing to make the trade, money for results.

Step Four: Price Presentation

You should have a price presentation that has several different options and programs. There should be a program to fit every budget from executives to students. The program should be able to meet the needs of all the individual goals. There are many different goals that the players will have. A few of the most common are getting into the pro leagues, beating the pesky neighbor, getting a scholarship in a college, and a basic introduction to golf as a whole. Your club should have packages priced from $50 to $5,000 and sessions that range from one to fifty. These are the standard pricing ranges and sessions that most successful clubs have. The presentations at your particular club will vary so you should check with your fellow coaches to ensure consistency.

Step Five: Closing the Sale

Your prospective client will give you the exact same objections that you will get when you are trying to sell anything. You will hear everything from "I need to think about it," to "I need to talk it over with my husband." Your closing techniques should be the same as with a training package and you should include everything from "TO'ing" to "price dropping" to "post dated checks." You will even use commitment questions such as "If I could get you a good deal would you want to commit to achieving your golf goals today?" You have to realize that personal coaching accounts for approximately 30% of the gross sales on golf courses today. Your members in the club are willing to spend their money and time because they are interested in achieving long-term results. Personal coaching is the most effective method the players can rely on in order to achieve those results. This is a very important aspect of what we do and if you cannot master this area, you will never be a complete professional, and you will be left behind in our industry.

Chapter 11

MY PERSONAL COACHING SCRIPT

"The best victory is when the opponent surrenders of its own accord before there are any actual hostilities... It is best to win without fighting." – Suntzu

MEMORIZE, UTILIZE, MAXIMIZE YOUR SUCCESS

Mr. Prospect, the starting point of personal coaching is goal setting. It's about setting a target of what you want to achieve because if you can't see your target, how are you going to hit it? Right?

Have you ever set goals before? What your coach is going to do is set challenging, believable, achievable goals within a specific time frame, and then put them down on paper so now they become measurable.

A proper swing accounts to 50-60% of your success. An extra yard added by your swing will mean an extra yard you are nearer to the hole. This is vital as the objective of golf is to get your ball into the hole. How is your swing right now? Are you achieving the maximum distance with your current swing techniques? What your coach will do is teach you the proper swing methods used by professional PGA golfers. They will also teach you the proper stretching techniques to loosen up the muscles around your hips in order to achieve the maximum results. Another thing they will teach you are exercises which will put more strength into those muscles needed to add that extra yard.

The third aspect of ensuring your results is the accountability factor. What that means to you is that you will be much more likely to come down to the facility and have a quality session when you have an appointment set with a certified professional. If for any reason you don't make it in, your coach will be calling you saying, "We can't accomplish your goals if you're not here!" Can you see how that will benefit you?

Accountability over time turns into consistency. We know that in anything, if we are not consistent, we are not going to be successful. Your coach ensures that you adhere to your regular practice in order to accomplish your goals. We recommend that you meet with your coach two to three days per week for optimal results. How many days will you be able to commit to working with your coach?

Now, motivation ties into this because your coach instills in you a greater degree of commitment to accomplishing your goals. Motivation is the difference between accelerated results and just kind of moving along at a slow rate and I'm sure you're like everyone else and you prefer results sooner rather than later, right?

Proper grip is also vital when you are going to drive that extra yard. If you do not have proper grip no amount of strength will help you improve. Imagine what may happen if you swing as hard as you can and you do not have a firm grip on your club. The club may end up traveling further than your ball.

Now, the "personal" in personal coaching comes in with program design. This involves your coach designing a customized program for you, and monitoring how you improve and successfully respond, so you maximize every swing, putt, and minute spent on the golf coarse to achieve your goals.

Price Prezo

Now, Mr. Prospect, normally a session of personal coaching offered by our pros is going to run you $70 per session, but what the company has done to make them more affordable for you as a member is they have grouped them into packages to suit your specific needs. As you can clearly see, the more you show that you are committed to achieving your golf goals, the lower the rate per session. The first option is great; it's what I call the starter package. It gives you some time to gain knowledge, learn techniques and how to apply them on the course so that you can continue to work toward being successful.

Now, Mr. Prospect, I'm going to skip this package for now and move on to what I call our accelerated results package. As you can see, when you enroll in a 32-session package with a coach, the rate drops all the way down to $49 per session. The great thing is that this is the one that our most successful players are a part of. This package will put you in the optimal position to achieve your golf goals through a longer-term commitment and you take advantage of the lowest rate. So you can see that this package is obviously the best value, right? You will really see substantial changes in your golf game with this package.

Now, I skipped the 16-session package for a very simple reason, Mr. Prospect. This is the most popular package when people enroll in the program on a first-time basis. It's the one that most people in your position go with. It's great because you get a considerably reduced rate and a substantial period of time to work with the coach and experience the true benefits of the program. During this time you will observe positive results and continued progress.

Now, I will back you in any decision that you make today toward accomplishing your goals. Out of the different options, which one would you be leaning towards?

One on One
SINGLE SESSION RATE $70

STARTER PACKAGE	MOST POPULAR	ACCELERATED RESULTS
6 SESSIONS	16 SESSIONS	32 SESSIONS
60 PER SESSION	55 PER SESSION	49 PER SESSION

GOAL SETTING
PROPER FOOD INTAKE
ACCOUNTABILITY
CONSISTENCY
MOTIVATION
PROPER TECHNIQUE
PROGRAM DESIGN

#1 Golf

Chapter 12

INTRODUCTION TO THE PRESCRIPTIVE PRESENTATION

After you have taken your potential client through a golf orientation, they should have some understanding of the benefits of the program. Make sure that you are sitting down and then take a moment to review the orientation card. This way you may refer to and clarify any of the notes that you had taken out on the greens. After finishing a brief outline of the results, it is time for you to use your six-step presentation. **This is a very pivotal moment and your success depends upon your diligence in preparation. Do you know the presentation word for word? The difference between success and failure will, in most cases come from ones ability to prepare.**

The first part of the presentation should be the benefits building process. The script that I recommend will follow the steps that I have outlined in Chapter 11 and will add value to your presentation. The following is a script that was developed by the same golf coach and regional supervisor at one of the pioneering golf clubs in California. The revenue and service produced by his golf teams still stand up to any modern day challenges. This script has been modified by thousands of golf clubs world-wide who have used it to produce and generate income from their personal coaching departments. Although, I do not endorse or use this script in my clubs, it definitely works. As a person in a management position and as a part of a team, I have always felt that it is important to follow a company system. I have worked in many golf courses that have used this golf presentation with great success. Whenever I found myself in a position where a company used or endorsed this presentation I used it as my only form of selling technique.

Again, it is important to have a presentation that helps the player to realize what they are paying their hard earned money for. Therefore, you have to paint a picture in a person's mind of the benefits they will be receiving from your service. If the benefits outweigh the monetary investment, your member or player will be willing to make the trade, money for results.

"No golfer can ever become too good to practice." – May Hezlet

Closing the Sale

Your prospective client will give you the same objections that you will likely hear when you are trying to sell a golf course membership. You will hear everything from "I want to try it out on my own," to "I want to think about it," or "I need to speak to my spouse." It is important to understand that as we are selling anything, especially sales in a golf club, your "be back" sales ratio will be very low. Studies have shown that 60% of customers will say no five times before they will say yes, thus it is important to try to overcome the objections when closing the golf presentation. If you are a new golf coach, I would imagine that the most difficult task facing you would be getting and keeping quality clients. You should allocate a percentage of your time every day towards becoming the ultimate in your trade and you must remember to focus on all aspects of being a professional. It is not okay to disregard one area of your arsenal. This is a book on how to sell golf. It does focus mainly on selling and retaining a quality stream of income, but it is also a large part of the bigger picture and should ultimately improve your overall success.

Chapter 13

THE SEVEN STEPS TO A PROFESSIONALLY STRUCTURED GOLF COACHING PROGRAM

Mr. soon to be client, 40-50% of your success on the course can come from **Goal Setting**, especially if your goal is to be a champion. In order to see optimum results, your coach along with yourself will set a long term game plan based on your current level of technique. For example: if your goal is to be a champion, the coach will assess your current level the positive and negative aspects of your game and determine the direction of your future success. Do you see and understand the benefit of goal setting.

Proper grip can be a simple but important focus, it is where the hand meets the tool. Focusing on this aspect of your game may seem simple and unimportant but once you have mastered it, very little thought will take place. Do you see where the coach is focused?

Your swing along with your grip are key elements in a champion. The success and failure will come from focus and long term dedication to perfecting this area of your game. You will want to get with the certified coach that has the ability to set long term goals, and put them down on paper to achieve optimum results with your swing.

Stance, along with momentum will be a major focus point. A true champion will break down every aspect of greatness right down to the smallest detail. Your coach will insure that consistency, accountability and motivation are instilled in every aspect of your stance. Momentum will be a key factor and you can see how having a coach will influence that.

Your coach will focus on **course placement** to find and understand the level in which mathematics come into this game. In golf, you must know the numbers. Do you know the distance from the tee, do you know which club to use, do you fully understand when to use a driver or a wedge. Do you see the benefits a coach can offer?

The **mental aspect** of golf can be without a doubt the most important. The best day physically will be your worst day if you don't have your mental aspect of the game figure out. The coach can learn, point out and identify how the mental aspect of your game can affect your golf game. Do you see and understand how your coach can help.

Professional Assistance along with the mental aspect of the game, may be the most essential part of your golf success. Your professional coach will ensure success by manipulating the above six variables so that your game does not level off in regard to the game plan. Your coach will then change and adapt so that you may avoid plateaus and continue to see changes towards accomplishing all of your goals on and off of the course.

Chapter 14

PRESCRIPTIVE PRICE GRID

The price presentation that is used for prescriptive golf selling is based on the golf coach being similar to a doctor. The golf coach will lay out details about your goal. Then based on your goal, the golf coach will give you precise information on both the time, and amount of golf lessons that are required in order to effectively accomplish your goal. Once the coach has determined the amount of improvement that the potential client may be interested in achieving, the coach will then prescribe the number of times per week and the total number of weeks that the client must meet with the coach. For example, the coach may say "Mr. Johnson you said that your goal was to decrease your handicap by 3?" Mr. Johnson says, "That's right." "Well, based on our experience and studies, we found that the average person with your amount of potential must train three times a week with a golf coach. Based on my professional opinion as your golf coach, I recommend that you enroll in a three time a week golf program with a certified professional. Also based on our experience in the field you should be able to decrease your handicap in seven weeks. Does this make sense to you?" "Yes!"

At that point, the coach will ask; cash, check or credit card. The player usually appears to be somewhat shocked. As the golf coach begins to complete the paper work, the member or player may try to back out of the financial part of the agreement. Many times, just being assumptive will help create a smooth transition towards completing the sale. This is not my favorite or preferred way to present prices but it is definitely effective. I have spent many years in the golf club business and I have witnessed many things that work and are successful. This golf presentation works. It is up to you to decide which presentation best suits your personality and style.

EXAMPLE: x marks the spot for the days and weeks that the client must meet with the coach.

GOLF GOAL SHEET   NO# 1
GOAL_____100% OF YOUR GOAL WEEKS____ DAYS___

PERSONAL GOLF COACH SHEET   NO# 1 GOAL_____
100% OF YOUR GOAL WEEKS____ DAYS___

	Monday	Tuesday	Wednesday	Thursday	Friday	Saturday	Sunday
Week 1	X		X		X		
Week 2	X		X		X		
Week 3	X		X		X		
Week 4	X		X		X		
Week 5	X		X		X		
Week 6	X		X		X		
Week 7	X		X		X		
Week 8							
Week 9							
Week 10							
Week 11							
Week 12							
Week 13							
Week 14							

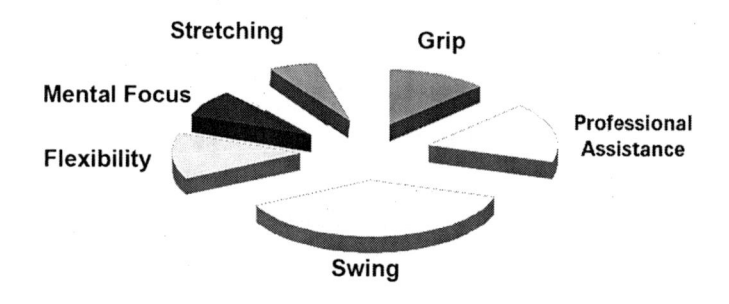

Chapter 15

THE FISHERMAN

The Fisherman

The fisherman realizes it has been a while since he has gone fishing, so he decides that on the morning of the following day, he will make a trip to the sea to try his luck during salmon season. He wakes up early, gathers his fishing poles and tackle box, and heads off to "knock them dead." He arrives at the launch ramp and decides to go to the bait shop to buy bait. Unfortunately, the bait shop doesn't open for another 20 minutes, so he gets on the water a little late. When he arrives to his spot, he realizes there are many other fishermen already fishing there. He is frustrated with the amount of competition, but believes there wouldn't be so many people if there weren't any fish. After about an hour trying his luck, he gets his first bite. He hastily sets the hook to no avail. Frustrated, he changes his bait and takes another cast. This time he hooks a large keeper; he feels like the incredible strength of the large fish may overwhelm him. He fights and he fights and right when he thinks the fish is about to give up, the line snaps. After changing baits several more times the frustrated fisherman hooks into another large fish, and after 20 minutes or so, he brings in his catch. Happy with his accomplishment he packs up his prize and returns home.

The Good Fisherman

The good fisherman realizes it has been a while since he has gone fishing, so he decides that on the morning of the following day, he will make a trip to the sea to try his luck during salmon season. He wakes up early in the morning, gathers several fishing poles, tackle boxes, and bait and heads off to "knock them dead." He arrives at the launch ramp at the same time as all the other fishermen and is the third boat on the water. He doesn't need to go to the bait shop, because he bought his bait the night before. When he arrives at his spot, he realizes there are two other boats fishing there. He baits up his fishing poles, and he is into fish after about 20 minutes. Since he has several fishing poles, he puts them at different depths. After about an hour trying his luck, he gets two fish in the boat. He is getting several strikes but seems to be having trouble hooking up. He decides that the problem may be his hooks, and he changes them. This seems to work and he brings in two more fish. Happy with his accomplishment, he packs up his prizes and returns home early.

The Professional Fisherman

The professional fisherman goes fishing almost every day. Fishing for him is more of an addiction than fun. It is a science. The night before the trip he grabs his fishing poles and changes all of the line. He rigs up and sharpens his hooks to a razors edge. He calls the bait shop to find out what time they open, what the fish are biting on, where they are catching them, and at what depth. He then takes a trip that night to the fish market to buy high-quality bait. He wakes up early in the morning, gathers several fishing poles, tackle boxes, and bait. With blood pumping through his veins, he heads off to "knock them dead." He arrives at the launch ramp and is the first boat on the water. Early bird gets the fish. He doesn't need to go to the bait shop because he bought his bait the night before. As he is motoring out to sea, the cool ocean air seems to increase his keen senses. He then notices the birds in the dawn sunlight are diving on some baitfish. He stops under the birds and turns on his depth finder. He lowers his already baited lines to the proper depth, and he is into fish right away. He is a professional at his craft, no down time, lines are always in the water. He has many fish in the boat in a matter of minutes. Happy with his accomplishment, he decides to try different baits, different depths, and different techniques. He catches several different kinds of fish and is happy to try new things. As he returns to the harbor, the other fishermen are packing up to go out and start their day. One of the other fishermen remarks, "Why don't you have any fish in the boat?" The professional fisherman replies, "If everyone keeps their fish, there will be no fish to catch. Catch and release keeps my love for fishing alive." He packs up and returns home early.

God created man to be successful, yet those who have died as failures could cast shadows on the greatest of pyramids because of their failure to prepare.

The Moral of the Story

The example I have described above can be related to everything in life. Because winning is a habit, losing is also a habit. Losers always lose and winners always seem to win. Losing and wining are equally difficult. Losers have to make up for their losses and have to deal with the repercussions of poor performance. Winners work equally as hard. The difference is that winners do their work and prepare prior to the end goal, and losers do their work afterwards to clean up the mess. One of my mentors once told me, "You can manage yourself by inspiration, or you can manage yourself by desperation." Both being equally difficult, you make the choice. The key points to create winning habits are outlined by the professional fisherman. His first and most important habit is preparation. His second is his love for what he does. His third is his commitment to perfecting his skill. Practice makes perfect. His fourth is his willingness to try new things and broaden his horizons. I wrote this story to help you understand or help you to think for yourself. Question: Are you the fisherman? Think about it carefully. Are you the good fisherman? Are you somewhat prepared? Or are you the professional? The whole package.

Chapter 16

HOW AND WHEN TO *T.O.*

T.O. *(take over)* plays a very important role in the sales learning process. Many sales managers and golf course supervisors will use this technique in the mentoring process. Many of the important and vital communication skills that are developed can only be fully understood at the table. Most of these skills are non-verbal and over time you will develop, improve and have the ability to understand all of the non-verbal codes.

This will not happen in a day, but in time you may look at someone's face and recognize when they are scared, not comfortable, or in a hurry. Only experience at the table will give you the instincts to tell right away if the potential client is not interested or in a hurry. Likewise you should be able to tell if your player just wants to come in and join and be capable of adjusting your techniques adequately.

This is what the TOing process is going to teach you. TOing is going to teach you what to say, when to say it and how to react in every situation. Usually when I am training new staff on how to sell, I will make them get up at least five times from the table during each sales presentation. I do this to advise the coach of the things to say and do during each step of the selling process. This coaching process enables the golf coach to fully understand all of the variables involved in being the ultimate professional.

Examples:

To excuse yourself from the table: "I will be right back." "Let me get the price sheet/business card for you." "If you give me one moment I can find out the answer for you." "Will you please hold on for a moment?" "Let me go and get a pen / calculator."

The player is not going to leave. The reason I ask new salespeople or coaches to do this is because I want to be involved as a manager in the selling process. I want them to inform me as to what is happening at the table. Some golf coaches go through the whole sales presentation and don't realize that the player has their spouse waiting for them, or that there has been a price change. Getting up clears the air and gives you the time and space to get advice, it also enables you regroup or think. It is somewhat similar to a timeout used in sports when things are not going well or to gain momentum. You can only learn so much from listening to yourself talk and you should use other strong closers and coaches to add their strong points to your arsenal.

What is lost when you don't TO? You have lost a chance to learn. You have lost a chance to make more money. You have lost a chance to close a sale. All these things are lost when you do not TO. When I was a new salesperson, I asked the other staff and managers to TO for me all of the time. This step was instrumental in my early selling success.

"Defeat is not defeat unless accepted as reality in your own mind!"

The most important rule of the T.O.

You *cannot talk!* You cannot say anything. Listen, watch, learn, and feel the energy. The only time you should talk is when your potential client tells a lie to the person who is TOing for you, but this is rare. Ensure that your guest is sitting down as you will rarely sell a personal coaching package if your potential client is standing up. It is imperative to practice and prepare in regard to getting a player to sit down, this will strengthen your closing abilities. Here are some basic rules when TOing.

Rule 1: It is better to TO too early than too late. Do not wait until the player is leaving, standing up, or totally upset before you TO.

Rule 2: If you are a new golf coach, I recommend that you TO before you give the price. That way, your club supervisor will be able to gain the commitment from the player before showing the price.

Rule 3: TO to your manager, club supervisor or top producing coach. Theses are the people you stand to learn the most from.

Rule 4: Do not be afraid to get up. If your player gives you an objection that you cannot overcome, get up and regroup. ("Hold on just a second, I will be right back.")

Rule 5: Make sure the person TOing for you stays until the completion of the sale. The person may feel like the deal was with the person TOing for you, and may bring up new objections once they leave. (Many sales are lost because of this mistake.)

Rule 6: Make sure that your company is on the same page when it comes to giving information. The last thing you would want to happen is for the person doing a TO to give information conflicting with yours.

Rule 7: The most important rule: You never open your mouth until you know what the shot is! This refers to making sure the person that is doing the TO is aware of what is going on and does not come in and destroy your sale. A briefing prior to the take over will ensure this does not happen

Rule 8: Last but not least **never ever talk**. Once the TO has begun you have given up your right to talk.

Chapter 17

FILLING OUT THE GOLF COACHING AGREEMENT

"Practice puts brains in your muscles." – Sam Snead

Most golf coaches tend to lose their sales, right when they begin to fill out the paper work or agreement. Most of the time, the player will try to stall by asking questions. They are often hoping to find something in your answer they can use to avoid getting started on the program. Some people find it hard to fully agree to the financial terms. You will see many clients that agree with everything you say but then will then try to find excuses at the end of your presentation in an attempt to find a way out of spending any money or starting the program. Remember, the **K-I-S-S** rule **K**eep **I**t **S**imple **S**illy. If you give too much information, the potential member will find something in your answer that may give them a reason not to get started.

Example: an untrained golf professional may say, *We are going to get you up early and start your day off with a good breakfast, then we will do one hour on the driving rage, and after that we are going to get you going on putting training!* First of all this is not asking a **question** this is making a **statement.** The statement will give the potential client time to "think" of reasons why this won't work. This form of communication lets the client's mind wander! This counterproductive form of communication is the number one mistake made by trainees. In this situation the untrained golf coach thinks that what they are doing is selling, always try to remember *telling is not selling.*

Always fill out the top of any golf coaching agreement with the personal information yourself. If you give it to the player, they will stop and hold the pen and start to ask questions. As you fill out the personal information, you want to ask a series of questions that occupy the client's thoughts. If they are answering your questions, their mind is occupied. The thoughts that are going through the mind of the soon to be client are that of *your choosing!* It is now almost impossible for your new client to think of his or her own questions to ask.

For Example:

"It is great that you have decided to join our personal coaching program, John. John, could you spell your last name? What is your address, and your telephone number? John, did you want to take care of your training program by cash, check, or credit card? And you brought that with you today?" Simply hold up your hand in the shape of a credit card as you continue to write, and they will almost always reach in and grab their purse or wallet. If they do not reach for their form of payment, ask the same question again, *"And you have brought that with you today?"*

It is important to remember that many of the players you will be selling to, may be just coming off the course and were not prepared to make a purchase. Most country clubs will keep the members credit cards on file or it can be run manually at a later time. At that point, you need to get the client to authorize the training agreement. You do this by simply explaining the agreement while pointing out each area of the agreement with your pen. I always put circles or stars next to the area that needs to be signed.

I explain, "John, this is your golf coaching agreement, we have all of your personal information and you will be getting your copy in a moment. Your total investment today is (whatever the total). Your price per session here as you can see is written clearly. I also wrote the total amount just to guarantee that nothing more is charged to your credit card. To guarantee and lock in the discounted rate, just go ahead and give me your authorization there." If they hesitate, simply tap your finger on the dotted line and say, "right here." If they start to read the agreement, simply tap your finger, and say, "John, I will be giving you a copy, and you can read all the rules and details." Again, remember to keep asking questions until all the signatures are finished. "John, did you want to make your first training appointment today or would tomorrow be better for you?" The training package agreement should be controlled by you the coach and should never leave your hands. It should be filled out quickly while asking questions. After the player answers each question, follow immediately with another question.

Overcoming the EFT Objections

Many clubs will offer the members the use of a charge account and others give the members only one option of paying for the training with cash, check or credit card. Whatever the case may be, most clubs will allow the clients to pay for the training in installments. When the clients choose to pay for the package in installments it is important the make sure that payment is "secured." The word secured simply means that we can obtain cash that day if the client doesn't come back!

An EFT gives the club authorization to automatically deduct the amount for the member's personal coaching from either their checking or credit card account. This helps the player by automatically making their payment and keeping their training package active without the concern of making their payment on time. It benefits the club by having secured access to a check or credit card. This secured billing method is done electronically and uses little time or labor, which will save the golf course a substantial amount of money in the long run. It also shows the company's stability to potential investors and/or buyers. When I was new in this business I was so afraid of this kind of payment that the potential clients could sense my fear of EFTs.

Remember, a large percentage of communication is non-verbal. If you are afraid of EFTs, your guest will sense it and will not be willing to use this method of payment. Many people have had bad experiences with electronic fund transfers in the past, perhaps you are one of them. Using this system, there is rarely a mistake. I will give you several examples of how to present the easy, no hassle monthly personal coaching program.

Example 1:

"Mary, your personal coaching is taken care of monthly, and your bank will send our bank a check automatically each month, sound fair?"

Example 2:

"Mary, I know you have had problems in the past with automatic withdrawal, but wouldn't you rather save your money and earn interest on it rather than paying your personal coaching package in full? The new EFT system at our club is far more advanced than the old systems. It is the safest and the easiest way for you to take care of your training program. I can assure you that if in the unlikely circumstance you were to have any problems you can call me directly, and I will fix it for you immediately. Mary, did you want to pre-pay your package or do our no-hassle plan?"

Example 3:

"Mary, if you do not mind me asking you a question, what would be the difference between the two payment types? You having an EFT monthly for your training or coming into the golf course to pay are the same thing. The only difference for you would be if you did not want to pay for your training, and you always take care of your bills, right Mary?"

Example 4:

Mary says, "I do not want anyone to have access to my account." I respond, "Mary, the only one who has access to your account is your bank, and you are authorizing your bank to send our bank $150 per month. We have no access to your bank. Any mistake that would be made would be made by your bank and would be your bank's responsibility. Take a look at the agreement, Mary. It shows that you are authorizing only $150 dollars a month on the first of each month and nothing more."

Example 5:

Mary says, "I do not do anything automatically out of my account." I respond, "Mary, I do not do anything automatically out of my account either. But I think you would agree with me that the fees for my checking account are taken out automatically by my bank. Fees for bounced checks or overdraft charges, new check charges, or annual fees are taken out automatically. So I think we can both agree that the future is going to only leave room for this form of payment. Most companies are even deducting taxes automatically from our directly deposited paychecks. So I think you would agree that in most cases, this is our only option."

Remember that an EFT training program is more convenient for the client, the golf course, and you. What you as the professional must communicate to the client is that this form of payment exists for their convenience. Like anything else, if they see how the program benefits them and they trust what you say, they will be more likely to agree to it.

Chapter 18

HOW TO OVERCOME OBJECTIONS

"I never hit a shot, not even in practice, without having a very sharp, in-focus picture of it in my head. First I see the ball, that's why I've busted my butt on the range for hours on end and made changes to get to this point where I'm able to compete at the highest level in major championships. That's where you want to be." – Tiger Woods

The seven most common objections you will hear will be the weaponry used by the players to stop you from getting them results. These procrastination techniques have been used successfully for years and will prevent you from selling packages. The sooner you learn how to overcome them, the sooner you will be able to start to help people to improve their lives. Getting your clients enrolled in a personal coaching package will be almost impossible if you don't learn to overcome the following seven common obstacles.

- Spouse /parent (I want to talk to my husband or wife/Mom or Dad.)
- My friend is going to teach me.
- Time (I don't have it.)
- Try it out (I want to try it on my own.)
- Think about it (I will be back.)
- Group/Friends (I have a friend and we want to take lessons together.)
- Too expensive

How long will you wait to learn how to overcome this weaponry? Clients will use the above, as well as other objections against you on a daily basis. The sooner you feel comfortable hearing the excuses and overcoming them, the sooner you can improve as a golf coach. DRILL! DRILL! DRILL!

"60% of all sales that are made in the world are only done so, after overcoming five objections!"

How to Handle Objections:

1. Hear them out. If you cannot hear the problem, you will not be able to understand their concerns.
2. Feed it back to them in question form, "You want to think about it"?
3. Show empathy. "You want to think about it? I can understand you want to think about it. This is a big decision. Other serious people just like you, have felt the same way."

   Remember Three Key Words:
   Feel: *"I can understand the way you feel."*
   Felt: *"Other people have felt the same way."*
   Found: *"But what we have found is that once you have started your training program, it will be the best decision you have ever made."*
4. Isolate: "Other than thinking about it, is there anything else preventing you from enrolling in this package today?"
5. Overcome: "What if it was only $10 Per session, would you still want to think about it? No? So it is mainly the money."
6. Get it down to money. We cannot control what their husband or wife is going to say, whether or not they want to

try it on their own, or whether or not they have the time. But we can change the price. We can work with different package options to fit their individual needs.

Although it is important to use the steps outlined in this chapter, it is also important to know that there are other ways to close a sale. The first closing technique that I teach my coaches is a very simple one. It uses redirection and it is effective when dealing with the right potential client. If you are a new coach try the redirection technique until you have learned the more complicated ones mentioned in the following chapter, *Closing*.

Keeping the Focus on Price

"Out of the different personal coaching options, which one are you leaning towards?" *"I want to talk to my husband."* "Did you want to talk to him about the starter package, the accelerated results or the most popular package?" *"I really just want to think about it."* "Did you want to think about the starter package, the accelerated results or the most popular package?" *"I really like the starter package the best but I am not ready to get started until I talk to my husband."* "Did you want to talk to your husband about the price per session or did you want to talk to your husband about the total package price?" *"I want to talk to my husband about the total package price."* "What if I could talk to my boss and get you payment options so that the total package price is more convenient for you, would that make you feel more comfortable?" *"Yes."* If I could talk to my boss and break your package up into payments, would you want to handle your business by cash, check or credit card?" *"Credit card"*. "Great and you brought that with you today".

Most objections will center around money. Money is a delicate issue to deal with, so people will avoid talking about it and find other excuses to dwell on. You have seen the excuses above and probably relied on a few yourselves from time to time. Objections are common in this business and you have to learn to overcome them if you are going to be successful.

Chapter 19

CLOSING

I feel that most coaches would agree that the bottom line in a sale is closing the deal. If everything goes great, you've done everything perfectly but you do not close the sale, the former is irrelevant. If you fail to close the sale then it is irrelevant as to how well you did. Nothing was really accomplished, and no money was made.

On the other hand, if you do everything wrong, and you still manage to close every sale, then from a financial and results standpoint, you are successful. That is why people who are closers are held in such high regard in our business today.

We can compare this to the quarterback who comes in and throws the touchdown pass in the final seconds to win the game or to the pitcher who comes in to closeout the inning. The people who can get it done are the ones who make big money. No matter how you get there, the end result is to win. This is the reason there is such competition and why so many people in the training business, or who are successful in this trade, are ex-athletes who have thrived and excelled when faced with competition.

There are seven steps used by many of the top producers. These are the areas that when focused on will make the difference between closing every package and missing opportunities. This information is the Holy Grail of the golf business. If you follow the advice, you will see a marked improvement in the area of closing. Although I can offer you ideas on what to say, what you say is not half as important as what you do and how you say it.

I have TO'ed thousands of sales, and one of the common things I hear from the new golf coaches is, and I quote, "You just said the exact same thing I said, and they would not join with me. But they joined with you!" I always reply, "Although we said the same words, you and I communicated something totally different."

Remember to practice these seven steps. Reading them will do nothing for you. We do not sell golf to books; these important steps must be practiced in a role-playing situation. Think of it like a football player who studies the playbook. He must know the playbooks forward and backwards to be successful.

But simply knowing the playbook is not enough. He needs to put that knowledge to work during practice and games in order to perfect his craft. He must learn to overcome, improvise, and adapt to many different situations as they happen. You are the quarterback of your career. I will provide the playbook, but you must provide the hard work and dedication it takes to perfect it for you to be successful.

The Seven Steps to Closing

1. Close too often and too early rather than too seldom and too late.
2. You must be assumptive. (Always assume the sale!)
3. Use the force, 93 percent of communication is non-verbal.
4. Mirror and match, people feel comfortable with people who are similar to them.
5. Control the conversation with questions. Answer questions with questions.
6. You must overcome five objections. Most of the sales in the world are made only after the fifth closing attempt.
7. Do not be afraid of silence. After asking any question, be quiet, the first one to talk loses the battle.

Close too often and too early rather than too seldom and too late!

"Were you going to come to your first eighteen holes dressed and ready to go? Or were you going to need a locker and a towel?"

You want to close too often and too soon rather than too seldom and too late. You do not want to let the opportunity to close a big package pass you by. Closing too soon rather than too late allows you to get a peek at the person's intentions or to gage their interest level. I always say, relatively early in the close, *"Which one of these different package options are you leaning towards?"* The potential client will tell you which package he or she is considering, and I quickly say *"Welcome to personal golf coaching!"* It is quick and assumptive, but you may just find the person thanking you and going along with it. If it does not work, the client will usually let you know. It is a gamble worth taking because usually the client will take it as lighthearted and fun and not become too upset. Even if this does happen, you have succeeded in establishing a relaxed situation by making the person laugh. Either way, you are closer to your goal. Here are a couple more examples of questions you can ask to try and close early.

I see rookie golf coaches making the following mistake all of the time. "Out of these three package options, which one are you leaning toward?" The potential client says he likes the starter package. The common mistake that a rookie coach may make is that they will then ask, "Is the price per session too much or is it the total package price that you are more concerned with?" They have over-anticipated an objection before the potential client provided one. *Do not do this!* Do not put potentially harmful words in your guest's mouth. The potential client just said they were ready to get started, so do not give them the option to now say it is too much. When faced with this situation, all is not lost. You can still overcome this and meet your objective, but you have made it harder on yourself.

The magic "yes" is not going to fall out of the sky. It just does not happen this way. Very rarely does the person say, "I'll take that package." What you want to do is gain their agreement along the way with questions so they are no longer saying no. If they are not saying no, they must mean yes. Assume the sale; you can never close too early.

You Must be Assumptive!

Being assumptive is probably the best close in sales. Just having an assumptive attitude and saying, "Great, welcome to One on One Golf Coaching," makes the player think that it is what everybody does and will simply figure this must be how it works. A lot of the time what we do as golf coaches is offer the prospect an opportunity to haggle by not closing the deal right away while we have the opportunity.

I used to work for a person whose favorite close was to show the prospect the different golf package options and say, "You know what? I think this one is best for you." Then he would start filling out the agreement. As soon as the person started to talk, he would ask them a question. "Did you want to pay cash or credit card; your first name, last name, address?" and so on. It was so assumptive that he did not even give the person a chance to think it over. He would just start writing. Many times that closing technique worked. But it takes a lot of time to get to that level unless you are just a natural salesperson.

Use the Force!

Use the force to close the sale. This may sound ridiculous to you as a new coach but, hey, it worked for Yoda. You may think that selling is just pressuring people and talking them into doing something they do not want to do. Actually, sales have little to do with the words that come from your mouth. Think about this: If you were to go into a dark room with another person, is it or is it not a fact that that a person gives off heat? Is it or is it not a fact that that person gives off energy? Is it or is it not a fact that that person makes sounds when breathing or moving? You can even smell them. With no sight and no words, there are many other forces that can affect communication. Behind words, there are certainly many hidden and not so hidden forces. You can insult someone with a smile and it seems like a joke; joke around with him or her with a frown, and it seems like an insult. Only 5 to 10 percent of the message you send consists of the actual words spoken.

Here are some other factors:
1. The tone of your voice.
2. The speed with which you talk.
3. The proximity between you and your guest.
4. How loud you are.
5. Fear in your voice.
6. Your facial expressions. (Many salespeople blush or make faces, and they are not aware they are doing it!)
7. Eye contact.
8. Ability to remain calm.
9. The speed in which you ask or answer questions.
10. The clarity of your voice.
11. Respect level.
12. Using slang.

I think you get the point. I could go on, but I think you are a newfound believer in the force. As I watch my sales area from 30 feet away, unable to hear any verbal communications, I am aware of what is taking place at each and every table. My coaches or training package counselors will often ask me, "How did you know what was going on?" I simply say, "I do not have to hear what you are saying; I can see everything you are saying just fine."

Mirroring and Matching!

Remember people buy from people they like, and people like people who are similar to them. It is important to adjust style and personality to be in touch with your player. What does this mean? It means having the ability to change the way you act, talk, and the speed in which you react or walk, everything you do to set your rhythm in sync with the person that you are with. This is not something that I can outline for you. It is not something that is easy to teach. But this is an effective tool.

For Example:

If you have a person who is shy, you cannot be aggressive. If you have a person who walks slowly, you cannot walk fast.

This area of your arsenal can go much deeper. You have to be like a chameleon, which is a lizard that can change its color and/or shape to meet its surroundings.

Lead with Questions!

The person asking the questions is the one in control of the conversation. When it comes down to closing a sale, your guest will ask a lot of questions that they do not really care about hearing the answers to. These are stalling tactics. They are looking for something within your answer that would give them a way out. For instance, you are filling out the paperwork, and Mary asks, "Who teaches your putting class?" An inexperienced salesperson might answer, "Oh, it is Jonathan; he is one of our best coaches." Mary says, "I do not feel comfortable being taught by a man. I think I will just wait." This exact scenario has taken place right before my eyes numerous times. As you can see, if this question was *deaf-eared*, or answered with a question, this would have never become a problem.

Ask for the Sale Five Times!

One of the most effective turnovers in sales is to *go ask them one more time*. The reason is, people can give up or change their mind. Sixty percent of all sales that are made in the world are done so after the fifth closing objection. Count how many objections or concerns you field while you are with your next couple of players. I bet it is more than just two or three. Here is something to think about while handling these numerous objections:

- If you give up on the first objection (some coaches do) you will miss 90 percent of all sales you could have made if you could have handled the five objections.
- If you give up on the second concern (a lot of coaches do), you will miss 80 percent of all sales you could have made if you could have handled the five objections.
- If you give up on the third concern (most coaches do), you will miss 70 percent of all sales that could have been made if only you could have handled the five objections.
- Give up on the fourth concern (do you?), you are missing 60 percent of all the people you could have helped if you just had of asked one more time.

The point is if you do not have the natural ability to help your players feel comfortable or to build rapport, or you fail to use the steps outlined in the "overcoming objections" section, you will never be able to get your potential client feeling comfortable enough to the point where you are able to field several objections without offending them. Remember, sometimes you just have to take the long way around. This may mean getting up from the table and clearing the air, or going back out on the course and re-explaining some of the facilities. Change the scenery for a while. Change the entire subject and try talking for a while about something that has nothing to do with joining on a personal coaching package. If you are too direct, you will never get to objection number five. Number five is the magic number. It separates the men from the boys, the girls from the women.

After Asking Questions, Shut Up!

The reason we ask questions is to give the client the opportunity to think of the answer. If you answer the questions you have asked instead of allowing them to answer for themselves, then you are not letting the players think on their own and they are certainly not being closed. You must be patient, ask a question and give the players as much time as they need to answer the question. Once they have answered that question you should be ready with the next question. Do not ever interrupt your player; the first one to talk loses the battle. Below is an example of a typical situation where you need to ask questions, wait for a response and then be ready for another question.

For Example:

"Mary, why did you come to the country club today?" "I want to practice my driving." *"Mary, if you do not mind me asking, your swing looks great to me, what do you want to perfect?"* "I just saw Mary play last night and feel inspired to make my swing better." *"How did you feel when you saw her yesterday?"* "I couldn't believe it! I decided right then and there that tomorrow I was going to play as well as her." *"Mary, if I could show you the perfect program to help you drive further and feel great about yourself in the shortest time possible, would you be interested in getting started today?"* "Absolutely!" *"Mary, did you want to go ahead with the package that included our personal coaching and course strategy or would you just prefer to go with our basic training program today?"* "I will take the coach and the course strategy." *"Welcome to one on one golf coaching."*

Closing Types:

The Verbal Closing: "If I could, would you?"

Of all the closes I can think of, this one is still one of the best. It is, "If I could, would you..." This means that if I could get that for you today would you want to get started. You always want to be two steps ahead of the other salespeople.

For Example:

"You know, we used to have this program. I do not know if I can still get it for you, but I can talk to my manager. I don't know if he will go for it, but if I could *talk to him and see if I could get that for*

you, would you *be interested in getting started today?"*

In many cases you will show the potential client your training options and they will say they want to think about it. What you need to do is mention the package that was just available, but has since expired. Then you can offer the "if I could, would you" close.

"Out of the different personal coaching packages which one are you leaning towards" "I need to think about it!" *"I can understand you want to think about it but if you were to pick one, which one would it be?"* "Probably the middle one." *"You know we had a special package option for that particular program, but it has expired! Earlier today my boss authorized one of these for one of our VIP members, if I could go talk to my boss and get this kind of option would you be interested.* "What was the special price?" *"It was 16 sessions at $40 per session. I could ask my boss. I'm not making any promises but the worst thing he can do is say no?"* "Go ask?" *"If my boss says yes how will pay cash or credit card?"* "Cash!" *"And you brought that with you today"?*

Two sales, One guest

This close I am going to tell you in story form. I see so many golf coaches make the mistake of not taking the opportunity of turning one sale into two or three sales. This happens because of a very simple reason: They never ask for it. I travel back and forth from the United States to Taiwan on a regular basis. Since I live in Nevada, I usually have a layover in San Francisco. There is a young boy there who is great at shining shoes. He is a master at his trade. He puts a lot of flair into the art of shoe shining.

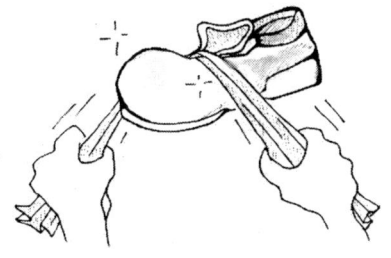

As I arrive at the San Francisco Airport, I see that he is working. I go over to him and ask him how much it is for a shoeshine. He replies by saying, "All of the other shine boys charge $2.50. If you want a shine from me, it is going to cost you $3. It is a little more but I guarantee you, you will know where that extra 50 cents went."

Selling Golf

Then he turns his eyes down towards my shoes, and he says, "Those look like a pair of expensive shoes." I say, "Yes, they are. They cost a lot of money." Then he replies, "Why don't you buy a cheaper pair of shoes, like ones from discount shoe stores?" I respond by saying, "Quality is important to me. I believe you get what you pay for." He looks me in the eyes, smiles, and responds by saying, "Then I guess you want to have your shoes shined by me." I smile and take a seat in the chair.

He opens up his box and starts to shine my shoes. Each time the towel hits my shoes, it makes a popping sound. He has perfected this trick over the thousands of shoes he must have polished. He spins the towel and hums and appears as if he is singing a song with the friction and popping coming from the towel. He then looks down at the bottom of my shoes and says to me, "These are Italian leather shoes, and I must admit they are some of the nicest I have ever seen." As he comes to the finish, I can see he has done an excellent job shining my shoes. He looks at me and he says, "You know I have something in my box that they made just for expensive Italian shoes just like these. It may cost you 50 cents more, but your shoeshine will last twice as long. Do you want to go with the Italian lotion or did you just want me to finish up with the cheap stuff?"

By now, I am sure you can guess my answer. Just by the way that he phrased his questions and the confidence he did it with, I was sold. A professional salesman being closed by a boy. He then does something that most experienced salespeople often forget to do. He asks me how long my layover will be. I respond by saying that I will be in the airport for another couple of hours before taking off for my home. He then asks me if I have to dress up for work every day. I respond by saying, "Yes, unfortunately, I have to wear a suit and tie to work."

The boy then responds by saying, "Do you wear the same pair of shoes every day?" I say, "No, I have different colored shoes for the different suits that I wear." As I see the wheels in his head turning, he looks at me and says, "If you have other shoes with you, I will be willing to shine them as well. Not only that, but I will be willing to put the expensive Italian lotion on them for free, sound fair?" Without giving me the time to respond, he follows up by saying, "Leave your shoes here for me, go grab something to eat, and they will be ready in 20 minutes."

Whether I say yes or no is not the point, the point is that he asked. He turns one sale into three, and he adds 50 cents with the lotion. I am sure that not every person says yes, but if 25 percent of the people do, he increases his sales by a large percentage. Do not forget to *up-sell*. Who says you can't learn a lot from a child?

Are you aware of the fact that McDonald's Corp. increased their sales 25 percent by simply asking one question: "Would you like fries or a coke with that?" They took it even one step further by asking people if they would like to "Super Size" their fries and cokes. They take the sale one step further by changing their menus from having all the different foods listed on the menu to having meal deals on the menu. Instead of having to pick just the hamburger or just the french-fries, they all come together in a meal for one low price.

The Lost Sale Close

The *lost sale* close is one you can use when your potential client is in the parking lot. It is a last ditch effort when everything else has failed. It starts with first letting the player know that you are aware they are not going to join on a package today but you were just letting them know that this is how you earn a living. Tell them that their feedback is important to you improving your craft and ask them some questions.

For Example:

"What did I do wrong? I must have done something wrong? I can't help anyone get started. I just want to help people and no one wants to help themselves. Is it me? Is something wrong with me? Did I do something to offend you? Maybe I am just not cut out to help people. Maybe those other coaches inside were right. Maybe I should quit being so nice and just start taking people's money. Forget about their goals and dreams."

I know, I know, it is a pretty low move. It is also pretty shameless, but believe it or not, this method does work from time to time. Hopefully you do not find yourself in any situations where you have to resort to a tactic like this. If you do find yourself in that situation, it is good to have a script ready.

Keeping the Focus on Price

"Out of the different personal coaching options, which one are you leaning toward?" "I want to think about it." *"Did you want to think about the starter package, the accelerated results or the most popular package?"* "I really just want to think about it." *"Did you want to think about the starter package, the accelerated results or the just the most popular package?"* "I really like the starter package the best but I am not ready to get started until I talk to my husband." *"Did you want to talk to your husband about the price per session or did you want to talk to your husband about the total package price?"* "I want to talk to my husband about the total package price." *"What if I could talk to my boss and get you payment options so that the total package price is more convenient for you, would that make you feel more comfortable?"* "Yes." *"If I could talk to my boss and break your package up into payments, would you want to handle your business by cash or credit card?"* "Credit card". *"You brought that with you today?"*

The Alternate Choice

The *alternate choice* is what we do when we show the potential client all of the different package options and then say, "Would you want to go with option one or would you prefer option two? Out of the different options which one are you leaning toward? Did you want to start today or would tomorrow be better for you? Do you want your training package with a male coach or a female coach?"

The alternate choice is a simple and effective close. In sales, you will learn that if you give somebody two choices they are going to take one of them. "Did you want to go with cash, check or credit card?" It has been around forever and works in all types of businesses. Learn it and get used to it because you will see that you will probably use this close as much as, if not more than any other.

The Ben Franklin Close

This close is especially good for a personal coaching package. It involves developing a plus *vs.* minus system. This close does not necessarily have to be a golf course close as it can be used for anything that you are trying to sell. What really matters is that you have the positives and the negatives of why the potential client should make a decision. It is very effective but do not be afraid if it takes a while as you may have to go through a little bit of a process in order to make this happen.

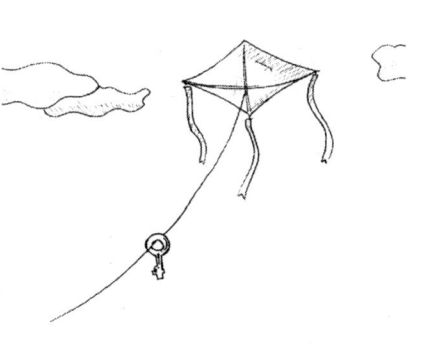

Ben Franklin, one of our countries founders had to make a number of complicated decisions and fortunately for us, he was a smart man. Whenever Ben Franklin had to make a difficult decision he would list the positives and the negatives of why he should make that decision. He would make a list of all the reasons why he should do it and all the reasons why he should not do it. Based on the positives against the negatives, he would weigh it out and decide if he should make the decision or wait for a while before deciding. If the positives outweighed the negatives, he would make that decision and *vice versa*. If there were a clear distinction between the two then he would choose the one with the most points in its favor, be it positive or negative.

It is really quite simple, all you need to do is write the answers to questions given by the customer onto a piece of paper. Title one side of the paper, *Positives* and the other side of the paper, *Negatives*. Ask the customer, "What positives do you think will come from you becoming involved in golf training?" The answers will vary and include such things as swing, grip, putting, club selection, stance, and so on. If they do not come up with enough give them a couple of more positives so you can fill up that column. Do not give them too many because you want them to see their answers on the paper. After writing down about ten to twelve positives, move over to the negatives. Ask the customer, "What are some of the negatives you can see as a result of getting involved in golf training?" The funny thing about the question is that there is no acceptable answer to it.

Whatever you do, do not help them fill out this side of the paper, they will have a hard enough time finding any answers so do not help them. You will receive answers such as, "I don't have the time" or "I don't have the money," two of the easiest objections to overcome. That is about it. You have not only showed them that the positives outweigh the negatives, you have also uncovered a couple of objections. Your next step is to read back all of the positives and then the negatives.

Your closing question will be something like, "Mary, wouldn't you agree that sacrificing an average of one hour of your time and few bucks is a small price to pay to be able to play better golf and enjoy your time on the course more?" (Simply read back their positives.)

You have now made it obvious that their objections have been squashed underneath the pressure of all of the positives they are going to receive. You have built value within the product, and shown that they need to listen to you in order to achieve their goals, that the only way to get all of the positives is to get started on the program. Once they have seen that, they will find it hard to say no because it is simply not a logical answer. It takes a little longer than some of the other closes but it is well worth it.

The Negative Take-Away Close

I found that this close works extremely well with a person that shows little interest or emotion. You have to find something in this individual that will stimulate action. I found that sometimes the only way to do this is by taking something away. You may find that your player says that they are not really interested in getting started on a package. They are not really interested in golf perfection, and they never thought about golf training before.

It is going to be hard for you to gain commitment if you cannot get your player's attention. You may simply state that it is okay, and that even if they wanted to get started on a package today, it would be impossible for you to sign them up. Tell them that unfortunately, at this time, the club is full of members that care about training. You may recommend putting them on a waiting list and giving them a call back when there is an opening for you to take more clients.

This may spark something in them that makes them want something they cannot have. The player may be using this technique to try to get you to beg them to get started. When you do not show interest, they will be surprised. This will cause them to loosen up on their objections and force them to show an interest in order to get what you will not give them. In many cases the prospective client will try to buy their way through the waiting list.

Magic Potion

I use this close quite often for the person that believes that there are shortcuts to becoming a proficient golfer. Trendy golf techniques, Infomercial golf clubs, become a pro overnight books. All of these are worthless with out hard work and proper training, yet people still waste their time trying them. You have to use a little bit of imagination, and you have to have somewhat of a good rapport with your player. Ask your player to think of a time when they were playing the best golf of their life. Make them think about the time when they were winning, looked great on the course, and people would comment on their golfing accomplishments. Then I would pick up a cup or a bottle of white out and I would look at the player and say, "What if I had a magic potion, and that magic potion you could drink and in the morning when you wake, you would have the perfect golf game? If I had a potion like that, how much do you think I would be able to sell it for?" You can ask your player, "If I had a potion like that, how much will you be willing to pay for it?" Your player may respond by saying, "That would be priceless. You can sell it for any amount." I respond by saying, "So you would agree that your golf game is also priceless? You and I both know there is no quick fix, there is no magic potion. Believe me. The only way for you to have the perfect golf game is to adjust your lifestyle to include your priceless game."

The Magic Potion close works to get the player to understand that there is no easy way to improve your golf game. This close must be done with those whom you have built a strong rapport. If you try it with someone who you do not have a good rapport with, they will not follow along and will miss the point of the presentation.

Benefits Not Bashing

One of the most important techniques used in sales today is focusing on the benefits. How is our product going to benefit the customer? Why it is important for the customer to have the product? Why does the customer need it? How does our product differ from other products? All of these questions need to be addressed before you are going to make a successful sale. The goal is to cut down on everything but the pure benefits. It is important to use our three-step method, statement of fact, two to three questions and a tie-down.

For Example:

"John, now I have explained the benefits of our personal coaching program, I think you would agree that no other coach can offer you a program to compare with mine." It is important not to knock other coaches; it can ruin your credibility. When a player talks about the benefits of another coach, I simply agree and say *"John, Tommy is a very nice coach, and I think you would agree that he has a very good price. But what I would like to do is take a moment of your time to tell you the benefits of my program, as well as the best price, and let you make the decision for yourself, sound fair?"*

By doing this, you are keeping the player interested in your abilities. You are allowing them to make their own decision but asking them in a way that only the answer "yes" will benefit them. Remember, you are there to make them happy. If you are looking out for their interests and trying to find benefits for them, they will appreciate it and you will have a stronger rapport.

The "Thinking About It" Close

This objection is at the tip of every players tongue if they are going to give one. If a person gives you this objection, they are in a situation where they are searching for a way out of committing, most likely to try to avoid spending money. It is what we call a "secondary objection" because it is often used to hide another. When the situation arises, stay calm and remember this close.

For Example:

"I can understand you want to think about it. Other people have felt the same way that you feel. What we have found is that most people have already thought of everything there is to think about. Then what ends up happening is you go home, you walk towards the door, you pick up your mail, and you start thinking about the bills you have to pay. You go in and listen to your answering machine, turn on the TV, get busy with the dinner and kids. One thing leads to another, and all of a sudden, it is six months down the road, and you really have not gotten back around to doing what you originally had the best intentions of doing today. Every morning we wake up and have the best intentions of doing all of the things that are going to make our life better. It just seems by noon, or half way through the day, our mind has tricked our bodies into making the wrong decision, into procrastinating, waiting, or putting it off until tomorrow. I think you would agree, that the time is right, and now is the time. What better place to think about it? You have all the information that you need on the table, you have an environment that is free from distraction, and you have me here to answer all of your questions."

It is quite a bit to remember but it is the only close you are going to need in this situation. You will find that people will make objections, such as this one, just because they are afraid to commit to anything. When they are in a situation where they cannot find anything they truly object to, they will fall back on their old-reliable "I want to think about it."

The "What about this? What about that? What if I could?" Close

I have found that the most effective close is just offering the player different options until you find one that works for them. Most of the time, your potential client is not going to tell you the real reason why they are not getting started. They will come up with objections; instead of telling you that the real reason they are not joining the one on one program is that you, the professional, have not yet found a training option to fit their needs. I read a great book about sales not too long ago that really opened my eyes. Two salesmen wrote this book, and it only contained facts and figures on what motivated people to make a purchase.

They put hidden cameras in sales offices all over the world and studied what the key points involved in the person's final decisions were. More interestingly to me, was when they focused on what the different salespeople did in different situations when confronted with different objections. The two biggest factors were No.1, the salesperson never asked for the sale, and No. 2, they could not find an option that met the customer's needs. Many salespeople today cannot close a sale because they do not understand the fact that the one or two options that they are offering are not working for the customer.

For Example:

"Mary, this package option includes a one time total investment of 500 dollars, leaving your balance investment at only $250." "I need to think about it." *"Mary, let me ask you a question, is taking care of your package in full an option for you?"* "I still want to try it first." *"Mary, what if I could get you a smaller package that would give you an opportunity to try the training program, as well*

as a little more time to see the benefits that coaching will have on you?" "That sounds a little better." *"I have a 3session option for $120 and I have 5 session option for $200. Both of them would give you some time to see changes in your game. At the end of that your package will expire. If you decide you like the program, and you are seeing results we could talk about a longer term commitment. I think this may answer all of your concerns. Out of option 1 and option 2, which one would you be leaning towards?"* "Option 2." *"Mary, welcome to the one on one training program. Your address? Phone number? Would you be handling your training package by cash, check or credit card?"* "Credit card." *"And you brought that with you today?"*

The example I have given above shows that Mary really did want to get started. I simply had to find a package option that elevated her concerns and met her needs. This is very common in our business. Many times it is not that the guest does not want to enroll, it is that the guest has not seen anything that they really feel comfortable with. The reason most successful coaches and clubs have multiple package options is so they can tailor them to suit many different people and their individual needs. It is your job to find the best one for each situation.

The "Just Do It" Close

I hate to say it, but sometimes just saying the words, *"Oh, come on, just do it!"* will be motivation enough for some people to enroll. I do not know why this works, but it does. I do not know how many times this close has been used in high schools to get an under-aged kid to drink his first beer. The words, *"Oh, come on, just do it!"* work.

You must have a good rapport with your player to use this one. It is playful, yet effective. Many people simply need to have somebody there to give them that extra shove to get them going.

My Uncle Close

"John, I know that you are not interested in making a decision today. You know there is a little story I would like to tell you, it would only take a minute of your time if you do not mind. I wanted to tell you the reason I had for getting into this business. When I was in my early 20s, I was still very active in sports and was very serious about making it to the golf club on the daily basis. At the time, I was concerned with improving my golf game and maybe hitting the big time in the PGA At that time, I had an uncle who was in his mid 40s, and was an avid but poor golfer. He practiced long hours daily and played 3 days a week, but never ever hit a score below 90. I would stop by his house on my way to the golf club and ask him, 'Uncle Tom, why don't you go to the golf club with me today? There are lots of other people there just like you, and maybe we might get a game in.' He would always respond by saying, 'I am busy working on my putting in the backyard, or 'Not today, I will go with you when I am ready.' he would give me every excuse in the book.

As the years went by, he finally gave up on golf altogether. So finally one day, I walked in his house, I put him in a headlock, and literally dragged him, kicking and scratching into the club with me. After a single lesson with one of the pros. He hit a score of a high 70. he spoke to some other seniors in the club that were taking lessons and made many new friends and golfing buddies that day. After leaving the course I asked him how he felt and he told me that he never thought that he would ever hit a score of 70 in his lifetime. My uncle has since continued training with the pro I recommended three times a week for the past seven years, and he missed out on qualifying for the USPGA seniors open last year by a single stroke.

To this day he still reminds me of the day I literally dragged him to the golf course to sign up for a personal coaching and regrets the day he ever let his pride get in the way of him improving his golf game."

Overcoming Objections

I am going to give you two or more ways to overcome each of the objections.

Selling Golf

"Spouse (I want to talk husband or wife, Mom or dad.")

Option 1

"I want to talk to my wife." "You want to talk to your wife?" *"Yes we have an agreement, whenever we do anything in regards to money we talk it over!"* "I can understand that, I am married too and this is a big decision. I know you wouldn't even be considering talking to your wife if you weren't **very** serious. Let me ask you one question, other than talking to your wife is there any thing else holding you back from getting started to day?" *"No."* "Let me ask you this Larry, if the personal coaching package was three dollars a session would you be able to make a decision today with out your wife." *"Yes."* "So you can spend money without talking to your wife, just not a lot of money. Is it the price per session or the total package price that is too much." *"It is the total package price!"* "So if I could talk to my boss and get your package price reserved with a small deposit and you could go home and talk to your wife would that work for you?" *"Yes."* "How much could you put down today to hold this price?" *"Half."* "Okay Larry, let me go talk to my boss. Larry, how do you normally handle your business, cash check or credit card?" *"Credit card."* "You brought that with you today?"

Option 2

"You go call your husband and see if he will let you purchase the package, and I will call my wife and see if it is okay for me to sell the package to you."

Option 3

"Your wife is going to say no?" "No, my wife isn't going to say no." "Well, she doesn't care; she probably won't want you to spend money. Is she is going say yes? If you are so sure your wife will say yes, then you really don't still need to ask her?"

Option 4

Your golf game has nothing to do with any other person other than you. Your husband/wife cannot workout for you or tell you not to improve the way you feel. Your golf game is yours, and it is 100 percent your decision. Buying a car or a house is different, because it is communal property. Your golf game belongs to you and it is your decision if you want to be healthier or feel good about the way you play. No other person can make that decision, wouldn't you agree?

"My friend is going to teach me."

Option 1

"I understand that you have a lot of confidence in your friend. I think you would agree with me when I say that going through a couple of personal coaching sessions can give you a better understanding of whether or not your friend has a training program that can get you the results that you are looking for."

Option 2

"I appreciate the fact that you feel that your friend is a great golf enthusiast. I should also remind you that our company policy requires all the coaches to have a certification and insurance coverage to operate in this facility."

"I don't have time"

Option 1

I usually quickly respond by saying, *"you don't have time not to!"*

Option 2

"John, you have already made an incredible investment in regards to the time and amount of money that you have put aside for your golf membership, if time is a concern, I can show you that I specialize in programs that give you more results in less time. Now you will have more time."

"I want to try it on my own"

Option 1

"John, I understand that you want to try it on your own; I also understand that you have had success in the past. Our new program is a relatively new concept and results can be seen in regards to what works and what does not. Some of the new information that I have to offer can help you get results quicker and easier and I'm sure if you are like everyone else, you would like to make your golf game improve faster and more effective."

Option 2

"John, when I was in my early 20's, I decided to take up golf. I went out and bought an expensive set of golf clubs, and despite the pro shop advice, I refused having a pro give me some pointers. In time, I developed a very interesting new system for making the ball curve when I hit it. When I finally decided to go in and see a professional to make an adjustment, it was extremely difficult for me to change my bad habits. If I had learned to play golf the right way in the beginning, I would have been well adjusted by this time. I implore you not to make the same mistake or pick-up the same bad habits that I did."

"I want to think about it"

Option 1

"I can give you three days to shop around. If for any reason you find any other package that offers better reliability or you like better, come back to get a full refund, and I can still give you a discount by starting today. There is nothing to lose!"

Option 2

"Mr. Prospect, you want to think about it? I can understand you want to think about it. I understand how you feel. Other people have felt the same way, but what we have found is that by joining on a package today, it will be the best decision you will ever make in your life. Other than thinking about it, is there anything else to stop you from joining on a package today?" *"No."* "May I ask you a question? How many days are you going to need to think about?" *"Two days."* "What if I could give you two days to think about it, and still give you a discount on your package by starting up today? I could give you a discount today and you would have three days to decide to keep your one on one golf package or get a refund. Sound fair?"

Option 3

If it is over the telephone: "I want you to go to all the other clubs in town, make sure you take notes about the different price options and services that are provided. Then, I want you to come to our office with the information. I will prove to you that our business can beat any other business when it comes to the services that we provide. Not only that, but I will also beat any business' price. I think you would agree this is the right way to make the most educated decision. Would morning or evening be best for you?"

Group/friends "I have a friend and we want to play golf together."

Option 1

"It is true playing golf with a friend can offer some great benefits, in most cases I found that in modern day society, with jobs and families, and all the things going on, sometimes being consistent with a partner can be impossible. Why don't we get you started with a 3-session package, and if your friend is interested, they can join us during our sessions."

Option 2

"Not only do I specialize in 1-on-1 golf lessons, but I also specialize in group training sessions. If you would be interested, I might be able to talk to my boss and include a program that would teach you and your friend how to train together and how to accomplish your goals in the shortest amount of time possible. If I can talk to my boss and teach you and your friend how to benefit from group training, how would you handle your payment, cash, credit card, or check?"

"It's too expensive."

Option 1

You can break it down to the ridiculous, most of the time it will be. "Your package is $200 per month, how much too much is it?" *"It is $50 too much."* "So $50 is stopping you from buying the package today?" *"Yes."* "Five dollars divided by 30 days equals $1.60 per day, so $1.60 per day is stopping you from becoming a better golfer? Don't you think your handicap and happiness is worth $1.60 per day?"

Option 2

"It's too expensive" is the best objection we can get. Out of all of the other objections, it is truly the one we have the most control over. We cannot control what their husbands are going to say, cannot control how convenient the golf course is for them. But we certainly have control over different personal coaching package options and prices available to them. You must learn how to handle this objection with many different tactics. If you do not, you will lose a large number of potential sales. You are going to hear it, so you better start practicing for it.

Option 3

"Out of the different personal coaching options, which one are you leaning toward?" *"It's too expensive."* "Was it the starter package, the accelerated results or the most popular package that was a little more than you were looking to spend?" *"I really just think that it is a little out of my price range."* "Which one of the packages is a little bit too much, the starter package, the accelerated results or the just the most popular package?" *"I really like the starter package the best but I am not ready to get started until I talk to my husband."* "Did you want to talk to your husband about the price per session or did you want to talk to your husband about the total package price?" *"I want to talk to my husband about the total package price."* "What if I could talk to my boss and get you payment options so that the total package price is more convenient for you, would that make you feel more comfortable?" *"Yes."* If I could talk to my boss and break your package up into payments, would you want to handle your payment by cash or credit card?" *"Credit card"*. "You brought that with you today".

You will get objections, everybody does. The best are the ones who have enough in their arsenal to overcome a variety of different objections and attitudes with a variety of different tactics and personalities. If you want to be the best, you must learn to overcome objections. The few that I have detailed for you will be the most common. Learn them, overcome them, and be the best.

Chapter 20
MY FIRST EXPERIENCE AS A COACH AND THE BOBBY JONES STORY

"All kids need is a little help, a little hope and somebody who believes in them." – Earvin Magic Johnson

As a new golf coach, you will spend many hours studying detailed golf swings and the human physiology. You may spend a substantial amount of time learning the intricate functions of the putt. As your education progresses you will learn how to schedule and juggle your different golf routines. After completing these difficult tasks, you will have an opportunity to go out into the real world. For most coaches this is the time when you may begin to observe your educational shortcomings and the answers during this difficult time may be rather elusive.

When I was a young student studying to get my degree, I had made a decision that after I completed my education I would go in to a sports or coaching type of career field. After studying for years and learning everything I possibly could about my field, I found myself getting ready to enter the working world. After doing some research, I found that the best fit for me would be working for a large golf club organization, one that had high volume, a good earning potential, the possibility of getting promoted and different locations in different cities. The most important aspect of working for a larger and more seasoned organization would come in the form of a comprehensive training program.

Selling Golf

When I started the process of interviewing and applying for different companies, the main focus of the employer had little to do with my educational background; in fact it seemed almost irrelevant. Some of the questions that were coming out of the mouths of the potential employers were rather shocking. The first place I went to apply was a country club and rehab center that had sort of a fitness style golf course in the back. It was well known and established and had a good reputation. I had a chance to meet with one of the partners and he told me that all the coaches had great earning potential. The only problem came from the fact that the job paid zero base salary and expected the coaches to work for free until they had built a certain number of clients. Not only was this odd to me, but the clinic also required that we pay for our own advertisements. The partner also stated that we were not allowed to use their customers as new clients! After determining this was not the best option for me, and feeling this was just an odd system. I decided to go to one of the large well-known golf clubs.

After going through an initial interview process with the head golf coach, I then had an opportunity to meet with the regional golf-coaching director. The first words out of the director's mouth was, *"Sell Me Golf."* I explained that I had not gone through any official sales training courses and I was not particularly interested in becoming a sales person. The regional training director told me that in a golf club, every employee in every department must have the ability to sell. After going to several interviews, I found that all of the different organizations that I was trying to approach had one thing in common, *making money*. After dedicating several weeks, and many frustrating hours, toward the grueling task of getting someone to believe that I could help golf club members get results, I determined that maybe being a golf coach was not something that was going to be in my future.

Upset and a little frustrated, and maybe feeling like it was time to give up, I decided to go back and double check the agenda and text material that had been such an intricate part of my learning process. Maybe I was sick the week the certification program covered selling. Maybe I was not paying attention when the teacher talk-

Selling Golf

ed about the needs and wants of future employers. After spending significant time on research, I realized the structure for selling and retaining or even acquiring new clients simply wasn't present in any of the training material that I was provided. Why would an organization dedicated to teaching such an honorable trade pay absolutely no attention whatsoever on how to make money or how to get a job. I decided that drastic times called for drastic measures. I had a close friend who had worked in the executive level of a large golf club organization. He had since moved on to other things, but had maintained a great reputation for being a top producer in the golf business and was still highly respected. I asked if we could meet and if he would assist me by answering some of the questions that I thought would help me in my quest to find out how these organizations functioned.

"Why don't other professionals such as physical therapist or chiropractors have to sell?" "Who told you those guys don't have to sell? The main difference between the chiropractors that make 100,000 and the one that make 30,000 is their ability to sell. Most of those guys don't even make it through their first year because they give up when faced with what you are going through right now."

"Why do the coaches have to sell?" "It may not be that they want you to be a great salesman, they just want to know that you are open to the fact that money is an important part of any business. A golf club or rehabilitation center is a business first and foremost. Nobody can offer a business service if they can't pay their electricity bill. Would you work for free?" I responded by saying, *"of course not!"* This answer really made sense to me"

"Why is selling such a high priority?" "Selling is such a high priority for the company because of the following factors. This is a golf club and the goal of the golf club is the same as those of the guest or the players, it is to get results. It is to get bigger, better, faster, and stronger. This is what kind of employees they are looking for; they want to know how you can help each and every player get results. Can you get a player results in 1 or 2 sessions? Can you get a player results if you can't get them to show up to their sessions.

Can you get a player results if you can't get them to change their poor life style? Can you get a player results if you can't get them to start working out? You have to be able to sell every aspect of golf or procrastination will win."

"Why do these companies pay so little as a base salary and such a high commission?" "In a golf club most people that work with coaches are doing so because they are not self motivated or because they want someone who will push them. Most of these individuals will not make the initial move when it comes to asking for the service. In most cases, even if they do ask they will procrastinate about getting started without a little push.

The golf course benefits the most from players that get results and this may not happen if the player is not encouraged by the coaches to get started on the training program. The commission pay system rewards coaches that actively recruit new clients and work with members to accomplish their goals. Also, if the club pays a percentage, the system will be fair and even in regards to the amount of money coming in and the amount of money being paid out." Everything seemed clearer to me now.

"Why didn't the schools teach you how to get a job or how to sell?" "The schools are a business first and the most important thing for them is to get students to pay the fee for completing the class, when you pay they make money. If the schools focused on selling or the hardships of clients not showing up for their 5am appointments a good percentage of the students would not complete the course. Lets face it, the realities of the business world are not always pleasant."

He went on to say, "Listen I don't have all the answers and being a coach is not just fun and games. You will have days just like in any job where things will not fall your way. You will have days where your boss will ride you for sales, you will have days where all your clients will flake out, and days where no one will buy what you are selling, you may even have your favorite client tell you that they are in love with you. Be aware that you are dealing with people and be prepared for all the problems that can come with that. My best advice is for you to understand that companies need people like you, and you are a very valuable resource. Go to the establishment that you think will be right for you, talk to some of the coaches and find out if the organization fits in with what you are looking for. You must understand that most large companies have put a substantial amount of time in to the systems that they trust in and use. They are looking for motivated individuals that will learn these systems, perfect them, and then take them to new levels once they have been fully absorbed. Be open to working hard at first and believing in company values, once that has been accomplished you can have your own ideas about how to run a large country club gof pro department. Maybe someday you will be writing the courses for the future training classes."

After meeting with my friend, I felt that most of what he had said made sense. I certainly felt that after the time and effort I had put into becoming a golf coach, it was not my personality type to just give up and throw all that education and hard work down the drain. I decided that it was time for me to confront my fears and find out everything I could about being a golf coach in the real world.

The first thing I wanted to know is why and how golf became the business it is today. As far as I could tell from my research, coaching in some form or another had been around since the beginning of organized sports. As far as my research could tell me, the trend of having golf coaches started in Hollywood. It was all due to a man by the name of Robert Tyre "Bobby" Jones Jr.

Bobby Jones was born in Atlanta, Georgia (March 17, 1902 – December 18, 1971). He was one of the greatest players who had ever competed in the sport, on both a national and international level. This was more impressive due to the fact that he participated as an amateur in a sport long dominated by professionals and blue bloods. Furthermore, he competed mostly on a part- time basis, playing only three months of the year. He also chose to retire at the age of 28, the typical age when most professionals hit their peak.

Jones, the son of a lawyer, was born into a well to do family who had a summer house near the East Lakes Golf Club in Atlanta. The young Jones played there from the age of 5 and soon demonstrated a natural talent. He was sort of a child prodigy and had won his first children's tournament at the age of 6, barely a year after first taking up the sport. At the age of 9, he became the junior club champion. By 14, he had managed to qualify for the third round of the U.S Amateur Championship. As a youth, Bobby struggled with his temperament. One famous incident was when he broke his club after missing a putt, and displayed such anger over such a silly mistake. Even though he never had any formal lessons, it was clear from a very young age that he had a natural swing which was so smooth and powerful, that professionals would later try to emulate it.

At the turn of the century, the Majors were considered to be the British and US Opens, and the Amateur Championships. Jones played his first major tournament, the US Amateur, when he was 14 and finished in the top 10. Jones hit his stride in 1923, when he won his first U.S. Open. From that win at Inwood, through his 1930 victory in the U.S. Amateur, he won 13 Major Championships out of twenty attempts, ranking him behind only Jack Nicklaus' 20 wins and Tiger Woods' 15 wins. Jones won the Open three times, the British Amateur once, the US Open four times, and the US Amateur four times. Jones was also the first person to ever achieve the double, winning the U.S. open and the British open in the same year.

That historic year was 1926. Jones is still the only player to have achieved the Grand Slam, which was winning all 4 majors in the same year. All in all, he won 13 national championships in a short period of eight years. In addition to those great achievements, he played in every Walker Cup since its inauguration in 1922 until retirement, winning 9 out of the 10 matches he played in the Walker Cup. He also won two other tournaments against professionals, the 1927 Southern Open and the 1930 Southeastern Open. Jones is also a lifelong member of the Atlanta Athletic Club.

Jones is considered one of the giants of the 1920s sport scene, along with baseball's Babe Ruth, boxer Jack Dempsey, American football's Red Grange, and tennis player Bill Tilden. He was the first recipient of the Amateur Athletic Union's James E. Sullivan Award, as the Top Amateur Athlete in the United States. He was also the first person, before the astronaut John Glenn, to receive two ticker tape

Selling Golf

parades in New York City, the first in 1926 and the second in 1930.

Though his talent was never in doubt, his health may have been at times. Jones was really skinny and frail in his earlier years, though he got quite plump in the latter stages of his career. He was never very physically strong, and had a nervous disposition, which he tried to counteract by chain-smoking on the course. He was also known to shy away from the gallery and sometimes had difficulty eating during tournament periods.

Most people would imagine that such achievements would have necessitated a full-time commitment to practice. However, Jones only devoted 3 months of every year to golf. The remaining time was spent acquiring first class honors degrees in Law, English Literature, and Mechanical Engineering. He earned his Bachelor of Science in Mechanical Engineering from Georgia Institute of Technology and a Bachelor of Arts in English Literature from Harvard University--where he was a member of the Sigma Alpha Epsilon Fraternity. After only one year in law school at Emory University, he passed the bar exam. When he retired, he set up his own law practice in Atlanta.

Not only was Jones a consummately skilled golfer, he also exemplified the spirit of sportsmanship and fair play. In the beginning of his amateur career, he was in the final playoff of the U.S. Open, and during the match, his ball ended up in the rough just off the fairway. As he was setting up to play his shot, his iron caused a slight movement of the ball. He immediately got angry with himself, turned to the marshals, and called a penalty on himself. The marshals discussed it amongst themselves, and even questioned some of the gallery to see if anyone had seen Jones' ball move. Their decision was that neither they nor anyone else had witnessed the incident, so the decision was left to Jones.

Bobby Jones called the two-stroke penalty on himself, not knowing that he would lose the tournament by one stroke. When he was praised for his gesture, Jones replied, "You may as well praise a man for not robbing a bank." The United States Golf Association's Sportsmanship Award is named the Bob Jones Award, in his honor.

Selling Golf

Throughout his time in golf, Jones had a very special relationship with the town of St Andrew, Scotland; although, everything was not always easy and smooth sailing at the St Andrew's Golf Course. He had a rough start to his career at St Andrew's. On his first appearance on the Old Course in The Open Championship of 1921, he withdrew after 11 holes in the third round. He firmly stated his dislike for the Old Course and the town reciprocated, saying in the press, "Master Bobby is just a boy, and an ordinary boy at that." He came to love the Old Course and the town like few others. When he won the Open at the Old Course in 1927, he wowed the crowd by asking that the trophy remain with his friends at the Royal and Ancient Golf Club rather than return with him to Atlanta. In 1958, he was named a Freeman of the City of St. Andrews, becoming only the second American to be so honored, the other being Benjamin Franklin in 1759. Today, a scholarship exchange bearing the Jones name exists between the University of St. Andrews and both Emory University and the Georgia Institute of Technology in Atlanta. A similar exchange exists in Canada between St. Andrew's University and the University of Western Ontario and Queen's University; the associated foundation is under the patronage of Prince Andrew, Duke of York, as a member of the British Royal Family.

Jones won everything in golf, and then he won it again. His career was short yet hugely successful. No one has achieved so much in such a short career. On that basis, he can easily be considered the greatest golfer ever. In addition, he competed only as an amateur and therefore demonstrated an unadulterated love for the game. Even today he sets the standard by which the greats are judged.

At age 28, Jones retired from competitive golf. In 1931, Jones started working on the first golf instructional videos, movie shorts that played in theaters. Jones later appeared in a series of short instructional films produced by Warner Brothers in 1931, titled *How I Play Golf, by Bobby Jones* (12 films) and in 1933 titled *How to Break 90* (6 films). Actors and actresses were mostly under contract with Warner Brothers, but amazingly, due to his un-waning charisma, actors from other studios volunteered to appear in these 18 episodes. Some of the more well known actors to appear in the instructional

Selling Golf

plots included James Cagney, Joe E. Brown, Edward G. Robinson, W.C. Fields, Douglas Fairbanks, Jr., Richard Barthelmess, Richard Arlen, Guy Kibbee, Warner Oland and Loretta Young.

Various scenarios involving the actors were used to provide an opportunity for Jones to convey a personal golfing lesson about a particular part of the golf game. The shorts were directed by the prolific George Marshall. This and the tourism boom that was going on in the U.S. at that time helped make golf even more popular. He was the one person who brought golf to the public. The popularity of the game was elevated to an unknown height all because of Bobby Jones, and with these instructional videos it helped the public realize that their game improved with someone actually teaching them and practicing the tips given out in the videos made them better golfers

This lead to a niche market for personal golf coaches. Therefore, every club professional who gets a paycheck at the end of the month should thank Bobby Jones for his part in bringing coaching to the mass media and raising the profile of golf way before a certain Tiger Woods came along. With Hollywood now in the bags many other celebrities took up the sport.

This was however, a time when golf was still known as a rich man's sport. His work with A.G. Spalding & Co. to develop the first set of matched clubs helped bring golf to the wider mass market and to everyday people. This, along with the opening of the railways tracks and golf tourism, caused many everyday people to take up the sport and start playing golf oin the courses that were popping up all over the country. People were able to play a different course every weekend due to the convenience of transportation.

Jones' fame is unquestionable but one of his highlights is co-designing the Augusta National course with Alister MacKenzie and he was one of the founders of The Masters Tournament, first played at Augusta in 1934. He practiced law. He founded Augusta National and the Masters.

Besides being a great golf player Jones also had an interest in writing. Jones authored several books on golf including *Down the Fairway* with O.B. Keeler (1927), *The Rights and Wrongs of Golf* (1933), *Golf Is My Game* (1959), *Bobby Jones on Golf* (1966), and *Bobby Jones on the Basic Golf Swing* (1968) with illustrator Anthony Ravielli.

Jones has been the subject of several books, most notably *The Bobby Jones Story* and *A Boy's Life of Bobby Jones*, both by O.B. Keeler. Other notable texts are *The Life and Times of Bobby Jones: Portrait of a Gentleman* by Sidney L. Matthew, and *Triumphant Journey: The Saga of Bobby Jones and The Grand Slam of Golf* by Richard Miller. Just recently published in 2006, "The Grand Slam" by Mark Frost, has received much note as being evocative of Jones's life and times. A few of these books stated are training manuals for being better golfers, therefore he is still teaching and offering golf tips to one and all form the grave.

Sadly, in 1948 Jones was diagnosed with a rare disease called Syringomyelia, a fluid-filled cavity in his spinal cord which caused first pain, then paralysis. He was eventually restricted to a wheelchair. His later life was spent mostly in a wheelchair and he never played golf again, though he continued to host the Masters. He died in Atlanta, Georgia in 1971 and is buried in Atlanta's historic Oakland Cemetery. He became a member of the World Golf Hall of Fame in 1974.

Jones was married in 1924 to the former Mary Rice Malone. They had three children, Clara, Robert Tyre III, and Mary Ellen.

In 2004 many years after his death Jones was the subject of the quasi-biographical feature film *Bobby Jones: A Stroke of Genius* in which he was portrayed by James Caviezel. The film was a major box office flop, grossing only $1.2 million the first weekend and $2.7 million overall, against a production cost of over $17 million. Sadly the film was also littered with a lot of historical inaccuracies.

Though his time in the world of golf was short, his legacy is still well and truly alive. As he is still referred to as one of the greats of the sports and his forays into coaching has affected more than one golfer as he was both a golf player and a golf teacher.

My first experience in the world of selling training packages came from working in a large golf club as a training package counselor, although I was more interested in being a coach at the time and had been involved in sports just about every waking day of my life. At that time selling golf club memberships was the position they had open so I took it, anything to get your foot in the door. Golf club membership selling was just starting to become something of an art form, something that only a very few incredibly skilled and highly trained individuals were able to do well. At the time, there were only a couple of companies that had more than ten or so golf clubs. Systems had not yet been standardized and most golf clubs had just recently started to develop a culture that could produce any substantial profits. This was the era that country clubs went from business to big business!

Before that, owning golf clubs was really only for people who wanted to play and did not care about offering quality equipment or services, this suicidal proprietor could never dream of producing a living. During this time, most golf clubs only sold a couple of items such as t-shirts and golf balls. A golf pro was something that was very rare, used mainly by some incredibly rich starlet. The golf club business had gone through a sort of metamorphosis in regard to the fact that they had discovered EFT.

This was a huge breakthrough that created a reoccurring long-term income from a business that had a hard time collecting payments. It was also a time when investors started to see the light on the possibilities of taking a small business and turning it into an anchor institution that would be needed by the average American. This was also the time when the computer became the norm in the average business or household. For the first time people had discovered how to do away with most of the manual labor that had been commonplace in keeping people fit. To be honest, the computer industry was the main factor for the increasing obesity of the average American.

As the golf club industry experienced a huge increase in usage, it became evident that people were beginning to realize that this was something that was growing into a necessity. As the business grew, it also matured into well defined and incredibly effective sales and marketing systems. As these systems were put into place, they were tested, tried, and improved by the people in the trenches, the gifted individuals who had spent many years developing a system that could work in a golf club. These systems were developed from a business that had everything going against it and was still able to create an income. Selling pro golf is unlike any other retail product. You have to think of the customer as an addict. This is the thing that most individuals don't understand about the business.

When a person wants something, they go out and they buy it. When a person wants to change their lifestyle, they will never do it unless someone helps them, the reason most addicts never recover is because they don't have the willpower to do it on their own. Poor lifestyle addicts are begging for relief, but they are not going to ask you to take away their best friend (poor lifestyle). I mean think about it, what person wants to change from pizza and beer, to chicken and rice and when asked that question, how many people are going to say yes to it right now?

The systems that I have used and embraced are the most successful ones that I have ever seen. I have been an open minded student of the business of golf for over 12 years. In markets all over the world and in clubs from small to large I searched for the most successful way to make selling personal golf an enjoyable experience for every person who steps foot through the door of a golf club from the front desk person to the owner, from the client to the coach these words and systems are gold!

Chapter 21
HELPING YOUR POTENTIAL CLIENTS KNOW THAT THEY DON'T KNOW

One of most common objections that you may encounter will come in varying forms. It is important to eliminate this problem before it stops you from closing a sale. In order to devise a plan of action for your player you must first get them to understand that they need your help. This is best done on the fairways as the last place you want hear "I want to try it on my own" is at the table when trying to close the deal. Develop a plan of action that will make your client understand that they need your help, do this in a manner that is consistent with your approach prior to the sales process. The most important aspect of helping the player come to the conscious realization is not an easy task. There are several steps that the player must go through in their minds in order to be fully aware that they don't know what they thought they knew.

1. The first step is the unconscious incompetence, that's where your player isn't aware of what they don't know.
2. Step number two is the conscious incompetence, that's where your player realizes what they don't know.
3. Step three is the conscious competence, that's where they have to think about it in detail before they are able to complete a set task.

4. Step number four is the unconscious competence, that's where an individual is able to perform a task with great ease and without having to think about it.

Knowing these steps to the human behavioral learning process, you will begin to understand and pre-determine a set path for preparing your player's mind. I have developed a system that I use for preparing the player to understand that they need my help. The system consists of a three-step process.

I use this three-step system in all of my clubs. It would be difficult for a player to not know the answers to all of these questions and still say they do not need any help.

Step 1: A statement of fact: *"We have 50 driving range stations. The driving range is used for improving ones driving to get a perfect tee-off. They are state of the art and have auto teeing devices."*

Step 2: The above is followed by two to three questions that will enable the player to understand that we have information that can help them to be more successful, and to accomplish their goals faster than they would playing on their own. *"John, do you know what your target handicap is?" "John, are you aware of the exact time, intensity, and duration that you should swing your club to achieve optimal results?"*

Step 3: Step three is a tie down. A tie down is a question that invokes a "yes" response or gains agreement from the client. To help me accomplish this, I simply nod my head when I use a tie down. *"John, it sounds like you may benefit from having one of our certified professionals tell you about optimum swing."*

I use this three-step system to describe several areas of golf training or equipment in my club. It would be difficult for a player to not know the answers to all of these questions and still say they do not need any help. Also remember that some small talk and rapport building is important during your orientation. You do not want to sound like you know it all. Telling your potential client that they need to lose weight or they need to get in shape will just invoke thoughts of doubt. I have found the art of selling personal golf coaching is based mainly on asking questions to help our guests think for themselves and make their own decisions. You stimulate their thought process through a series of questions and must remember to let the player answer each question fully and completely before asking your next question.

There is an old saying that goes, "telling is not selling." Wouldn't you agree? If you tell someone they need to lose weight or need to get started on a personal coaching program, they may believe you or they may doubt it.

If you ask a person what brought them in today, and they say they need to improve their putting, in that person's mind, it is true. The question, "What brought you in today?" stimulates people to ask themselves, "Why *did* I come to the course today?" After they answer your question, you may even want to follow up by asking, "Why do you want to improve your putting?" They may answer, "So I can learn to focus on my short game and improve my score." At this point you may follow up that question by saying, "How does that make you feel?"

These different questions will stimulate the players to think on their own. It is important to let the players make their own decisions based on their own thoughts. These thoughts can be stimulated through questions, not by statements and not by you telling them.

I have listed some questions that you can ask and the areas in which you can ask them, as well as some great tie downs to make your tours more effective. There are many ways to give a tour, and this is just one of them. It gives you the room to add your own style whereby you should try to create excitement and awe wherever possible.

Proper Swing Techniques

Questions

1) Are you aware that proper swing will help you reduce the number strokes from your game drastically?
2) Are you aware of the proper angle the spine should be at the end of your golf swing?

Tie downs

1) How would you like to have a club pro show you how to swing better and help you break 90?
2) Isn't it nice that we have professional coaches to help you eliminate the guesswork and design the most effective golfing program for you?

Good putting and grip techniques

Questions

1) Did you know that improving your putting is the difference between an eagle and a birdie?
2) Did you know the way you grip your golf club will be the difference in winning and losing a game?

Tie downs

1) Wouldn't it be more effective if a professional could help you eliminate all the tiny mistakes as he watches and corrects you from the sideline to help you win the game?
2) Don't you think that with a pro guiding you through the process, it would help you grip the club firmer and play with more confidence?

Mental focusing

Questions

1) Are you aware that 90% of games are won and lost because of the players' mental preparation before a game?

2) What mental preparation have you ever done before stepping onto the fairways in the past? Do you feel that you have won enough games with these preparations?

Tie Downs

1) How would you like to work with a club pro and let him show you how professional golfers get psyched up before a game?

2) Does it make sense if you are to be set up for success that you would want someone who has 'been there, done that' to show you how and customize a program to suit your needs?

Again, these are just suggestions. You are free to include some questions of your own. These questions and tie downs have been tried and tested for many years and have met with outstanding results.

Chapter 22
TIME MANAGEMENT

"Part of the reason why that I have been successful managing sales systems is that I have always kept the systems simple and I avoid using a computer. We are in a people business"

Effective time management is imperative in order to lead a successful life. Everyone from students, to housewives, to the CEO must have a structured system that creates good habits. I cannot stress enough the impact effective time management can have on your success in life. You only have so much time and when that time is up, your life is over. For many of us procrastination takes over, bad habits are formed and we never accomplish the things we want in life because we do not have good time management skills.

One of the owners that I used to work for was always quick to bring up a story about his ditch digging theory. He would say that one of his employees would spend all day digging a ditch. It was deep, long and faultlessly round. It was a perfect ditch. He worked hard all day and he was happy with his accomplishment. When he was finished, he would come back into the office and say, "I worked hard all day. I even have blisters on my hands and now I am finally done. Isn't it a beautiful ditch?" And the owner would reply, "Yes, you have worked hard and indeed it is a beautiful ditch. There is only one problem, we don't need a ditch!"

The story is to remind you that your job is to sell personal golf coaching and get players results. It is important to keeping focus *the main thing, the main thing*. Work smart, not hard, and stay focused on the business at hand. If your club is like mine, you only get paid for selling and completing sessions. Do you realize that if you spend

10 minutes a day saving money, 10 minutes a day learning a foreign language, 10 minutes a day writing a book and 10 minutes a day on building a house that in a couple of years, you would have saved a lot of money, you would speak a foreign language, would have written a book and even built a house all in under 40 minutes a day.

I relate time management to the prospective client sitting across from you during a sale. Every day you know you should do these things, but every day your mind tricks your body into "thinking about it," trying it out, into putting it off until the next day. That "other day" will never come. You will be an old person sitting around telling yourself, "I should have, I could have, if only…" My mentor taught me one of the most valuable lessons I have ever learned in this business. He said to me, "Have a five-year plan, have a one-year plan, have a monthly plan and have a daily plan." Looking back on this advice now, I did not always hit my daily plan. But I came pretty close. I did not always hit my monthly plan, but I came pretty close. I did not always hit my annual plan, but I would come pretty close. I think you know the answer to the five-year plan. Achieving small goals is the foundation for reaching large ones. Take baby steps. No step is too small, and no goal or dream is too big. If you have a plan and manage your time then your dream can be accomplished.

"There are two ways to work. You can work hard or you can work smart. I found the later to be much more lucrative."

My whole system is based on accountability and time management. The system can only work if you use it, and you can only use it if you manage your time correctly. Sit down with your manager or mentor and put together your goals. Once you have done that, work toward devising a plan in order to achieve those goals. In the end, anything can be achieved.

What I Should Do When I Get to Work

1. Walk through the Club House. (Meet and greet clients and check equipment for maintenance and cleanliness.)
2. Confirm Personal coaching appointments and orientations.
3. Update your statistics and personal planner.
4. Update and check the Master Appointment Book.
5. Check and call all new client agreements from the previous day and make orientation appointments, and use welcome greetings.
6. Schedule at least three orientation appointments.
7. Sit in on three new client presentations.
8. Go training with one other golf pro and compare techniques, role-play on sales presentations.
9. Check-out with your personal coaching supervisor and make sure your goals are achieved.

Chapter 23

PERSONAL PRO-LESSON RE-SIGNS

> *"The sales job is about opportunities. The more opportunities you can have, the more sales you can make! Lost and untracked opportunities are the acts of a fool."*

Re-signing a personal coaching client can be just as important as signing a new one. Not only is it important in helping your members to accomplish their goals, but also crucial in maintaining a steady income. Many of the successful coaches that have had long-term success do so through a steady and reliable source of re-signing clients. It is important to remember that many golf enthusiasts prefer to play golf only when they have a golf coach present. Developing a consistent system for re-signing clients will ensure a quality recurring personal golf coaching business.

Having good long-term success as a golf coach can be very rewarding. This can only happen if you are able to maintain a healthy relationship with your occupation. You should get along with your clients, that is, if you're forced to train people that you are not comfortable with, you may find that your job is intolerable. Loving what you do, or dreading the mere fact of even showing up to work, could all depend on picking and choosing a quality group of clients that you yourself feel comfortable with. Once you have established a quality group of clients, you may then begin to determine your hours, your number of clients, and even the rates you charge. These benefits may only be enjoyed if you are able to maintain and re-sign a quality client list.

I will give you several presentations that will help in your ability to re-sign a quality client list.

"Mary, I couldn't help but notice that you only have 3 sessions of coaching left. I'm also sure that you are aware that tomorrow is the final day for our closeout special. We have had incredible success together and I think you would agree that we want to continue in accomplishing all of our original goals. Your success is my success. I would recommend that you reserve your 8:30 time slot before one of my other clients tries to take it."

A golf coach has the unique ability to work with their clients on a daily basis, sometimes using a take-away close can help to set your self up for future success.

"Mary, I know that this may be an uncomfortable question, and I know that you like to go to the driving range after you get off work at 6pm. I have a VIP client who is interested in personal coaching and retaining my services. If you are not interested in re-signing on a long-term package, I may have to reserve this time slot for another individual."

As you begin to evolve as a golf coach and as a sales person you will start to realize that the two things are not separate, they are one in the same. In the beginning, it is important to focus on each separate area, but as you become more experienced, you may start to realize that selling is part of the job. My personal coaching re-sign presentation has evolved so far that I don't even give my clients an option.

"Mary, as my client, you agreed that you would put a 100% effort in accomplishing your goal. As your golf coach, I feel that it is my job to give you no other option than accomplishing your original goal. I have already filled out your agreement for another 20 sessions, this was a special package price that our golf course offered, and I told my boss to reserve 20 sessions at the discounted rate. Mary, do you want to handle your package by cash or credit card."

Selling Golf

It is impossible to get your clients results if you cannot get them to complete their training. The most important thing to remember in re-signing your clients is that you cannot wait until they finish their entire package, if you wait till the last session, you will have little success in re-signing. You should start selling personal coaching when your client has 3-4 sessions left.

Chapter 24

MASTER APPOINTMENT BOOK

The master appointment book (MAB) is an important tool used in country clubs and most service businesses. This important tool is the foundation for team production. If preparation is the key, then this book is the key to success. I believe it would be difficult to fail as a sales manager if you master the art of keeping your MAB filled with quality appointments and follow up on those appointments.

When I use the master appointment book, I make 30 sheets for the whole month and put the names of each golf coach on the top of each page. Each separate sheet should have the times and an area next to them for their names and telephone numbers. There should also be an area for the results. The reason we use the MAB is to track all of the leads and sales in the golf club. Then, through practice and repetition, we learn how to most effectively turn these valuable appointments into revenue. Be sure to track all of your individual appointments for the month, closeouts, and for the next day. You should write your appointments in the master appointment book right when you book them, or call up to the front desk and have them written in for you. Daily goals can also be recorded in this book. Remember to take notes and get more than one telephone number.

Let's say you take a telephone inquiry. Once you have booked the appointment you call the front desk to let them know. Make sure they write down the telephone number and the appointment date on the TI sheet. Then you write the appointment down in the master appointment book for the time and day that it is scheduled. Include the name, work/home number and cell telephone number if possible.

Your planner or personal appointment book should be your master plan for the month. There should be no appointments in any planners that are not also in the master appointment book.

The master appointment book also gives you a list of people to call, such as no-shows, missed sales, and so on. The first job given to a golf coach moving into a management role is to manage the master appointment book. The reason for this is obvious. If you can manage the master appointment book; you are managing the first step of production. *The rule for appointments is half show, half join. So if you have 10 appointments a day, 5 will show and 2.5 people will join.*

Two point five training packages per day will make you a successful salesperson. A good golf manager knows how to run and drive appointments. The master appointment book should be checked several times a day to ensure it is being utilized correctly and consistently. It is a tool that can be used to monitor the progress of the golf club as well as keep an eye on how the club is set up for future dates. "John, you have no appointments for tomorrow and only two appointments for closeout, and closeout is in three days." If you find that you are deficient in a specific area when it comes to appointments, you can have an appointment marathon. For instance, you can have salespeople coming into the telephone room for one hour and whoever makes the most appointments in that hour gets a free lunch or a cash bonus. You can have every salesperson make one appointment per hour.

For example; coming into the office at exactly twelve o'clock, everyone gets on a telephone and as soon as they book one appointment they are done. You will do that again at one o'clock and again at two o'clock. Each golf coach has to have at least four appointments a day. If you have 10 golf coaches, which will be 10 guaranteed training packages without a walk-in. If you neglect your master appointment book, your sales and production will be greatly lowered.

Production Meetings

The MAB should be checked in the production meetings for appointments every day, whether or not previous day's goals were hit, in order to set goals for the day. This is the perfect time to do this because during the production meeting all golf coaches should be in attendance as well as have their planners completely filled out. Anything that needs to be added to the MAB can be added at that time.

Chapter 25

WORKING THE FAIRWAYS

You must offer golf packages sitting down. I cannot give you a detailed explanation of why it is important to present Golf packages sitting down, but your odds of closing a sale increase substantially once you are sitting at the table.

The beauty of working in a golf club can come from many different aspects in our business. If you are selling anything from cars to copy machines to golf club training packages, the hardest thing about the job is getting the people in front of you. When I refer to the beauty of our business, I am referring to the fact there is a steady stream of customers flowing into our facility at any given moment. I see many training package representatives or golf coaches, who think that the only way to make a living is to wait for walk-ins or wait for their orientation appointments to show up. The truth of the matter is evident that all the business you will ever need to make a substantial income, is right in front of your eyes. If you have ever worked in a country club that does very little advertising or has very little walk in traffic you would have had to rely on other avenues to create your income. There are some very simple rules that can make a difference in your ability to work the greens. Follow these rules and you will never have to worry about walk-ins or waiting for the players to come to you.

Rule 1:

For the majority of the members that are playing golf, image is everything. Most of your members will not admit that they need help. It is important to understand that your members may not understand how to get results or even how to do basic techniques. This absence of knowledge may create shortcomings in your members' abilities to get results, as most members will not ask for help. You must understand that this gap exists.

Rule 2:

Although it is important to contact your players, it is also very important to make sure you are not intrusive. One common complaint that I hear from members playing in golf clubs is that they feel the coaches tend to be overly aggressive. When I approach a member on the driving range, I never linger. I may say something like "I noticed your technique and I thought I might be able to offer some pointers. My desk is right over here. And if you like, stop by to see me after you have finished."

Rule 3:

This rule has made a substantial increase in my ability to add creditability to my knowledge. I have a detailed filing system of articles that pertain to all aspects of golf and fitness. These articles may vary from a wide range of different topics on anything from medical conditions, to how to exercise properly. I have articles from supplementation to injury rehabilitation. It is important in any type of sale to give before you get. I may offer to make copies of the article for the player, the web sites for golf business or golf club management magazines which offer years of back issues and have detailed articles for the purpose of education.

Rule 4:

It is important to remember that you can offer a quick session. This would include going out on the driving range, offering a short session for no cost. The best time to go out on a driving range and offer some pointers would be NOW! Don't be afraid or hesitate when it comes to taking your player through a quick driving exhibition based on education, giving your member the service that they came to a golf club for.

Selling Golf

Rule 5:

Although most coaches spend a substantial amount of time on the education and on the exercise knowledge, most coaches will fall short when it comes to producing an income. Asking for money is part of being a golf coach. If you cannot get a member to enroll into a personal coaching package, you will have very little success in helping your members get results. It is important to practice the use of high quality presentations such as those mentioned in previous chapters, that have been tested and tried and have been proven to be successful. You should have these presentations memorized word for word and you cannot be afraid of offering your service for a fee. Most of the problems caused in regards to the selling process come from the player feeling pressured from an untrained, unprofessional coach using a broken selling system. The coach may be feeling the same pressure from not memorizing this kind of presentation, thus not being prepared. Practice makes perfect!

Rule 6:

You must offer personal coaching sitting down. I cannot give you a detailed explanation of why it is important to present personal coaching sitting down. But your odds of closing a sale increase substantially once you are sitting at the table.

Rule 7:

The last and most important step that many golf coaches fail to adhere to is the good old fashion art of asking for a T/O (take over). Don't be afraid to ask for help. You may just learn something!

Working the range for golf coaches can be a rewarding avenue for a higher income and increasing your client base. This endless source of people can be tapped into if you practice the steps that I have outlined above. Remember as a quality coach you must have the ability to recruit and keep quality clients, selling is part of your job!

Chapter 26

THE WALL OF FAME

I am sure if you have spent enough time to get to this point in the book, then you are probably like me. You are one of those individuals who spend a substantial amount of time on developing your education level. A good percentage of your time is probably spent studying written material, magazines or articles or just plain learning from other successful companies in our industry. One of the most successful authors in terms of fitness and its impact on the weight loss business would be Bill Phillips of EAS. He developed the book "Body for Life." This incredible fitness system was on the New York Times bestseller list for more than a year. Another company that has been extremely successful in terms of their sales and production would be Weight Watchers. As a student dedicated to improving our ability to recruit, sell and get results for personal golf coaching clients, we have found that one thing these two companies use in a very successful manner would be the before and after concept. This successful concept was used everywhere in the 70s and 80s and really seemed to die out during the 90s.

But now if you look at these types of sales or marketing techniques, you can see that many companies are going back to this proven success method for promoting their product. In my golf courses I set up a wall of fame. The wall should have lots of pictures; they should include before and after scores. With today's digital cameras this should be a cinch. The next step is the testimonial. This should come in the form of a letter and, the player should write it. It should outline the steps that were taken in order to gain success with the personal golf coaching program.

- What package did they buy? This is important because it gives the potential client some insight into what needs to be done in terms of investment and may relieve some of the anxiety about what package to get started on!

- How many times a week did they work with the coach? Working with a coach requires a bit of re-allocation and life style adjustment. The wall may relieve some of those concerns as well. It may also give your potential client expectations of commitment

- How long were the lessons and what did they consist of? The practice routine is very important because seeing the progress and the routine helps the player see the amount of time and planning that goes into the sometimes complex art of getting your members results

- What supplements did they take and what was the food intake like? Supplements and joint therapy have become commonplace in most training programs and if they are not adjusted properly the results may be slow coming.

- How many days off did you have? This will be vital to many of your players and the days off may be a necessity. Make sure to show that all of your clients may have had a day or even weeks off at some point in the quest for success and these set backs don't stop success. This shows the reality of the program and highlights your compassion to your potential client.

- What was the role of the coach? This is the most important part of the wall of fame. You have to explain the role of the coach and how the coach made a difference in the success of the program. For example, Mary stated that she had tried many different programs and this was the first time she had any type of long term success, therefore the coach was the difference.

- When did you first start to see score improvement? For many new personal golf clients the first sign of change is very slow and sometimes a perfect swing may take two or three weeks before any substantial changes occur. Again it is important to show new clients that they are not alone in this battle and that the successful clients had the same slow start. This is just part of the battle and if others have done it so can they.
- Show the before and after scores Show the numbers. This is concrete evidence of individual achievements. If you do a good job on the orientation you should have an outline of the before scores, the distance of the drive, the average hits per hole, and so on. If it is in black and white your clients can visualize their progress and feel proud.
- And be sure to include the obvious, how do you feel now? It is also good to let the potential clients know that once goals have been reached with the assistance of a personal golf coach, one experiences physical rewards. This is important. The feeling of success is something everyone can relate to and should be instilled with a plaque on the wall of fame.

The wall of fame should be put in a high profile place near the driving range and should be updated often. The message should be perfectly clear; if you want to be successful you should do what every one else is doing! If you want to be successful; get a personal golf coach!

CHAPTER 27

THE CLOSEOUT MASTER PLAN

Someone once told me the atmosphere at the front desk should be like Disneyland. Overly friendly!

As the ultimate golf coach, it is important to use all resources possible to develop and enhance your ability to recruit and involve clients in the program. The closeout master plan is a detailed outline of what it would take for you to develop an incredible buying frenzy. In this day and age, most golf clubs are familiar with a closeout party but there are still many golf clubs that do not believe in having this type of promotional event.

In the twelve years that I have worked in the golf business, I have never seen a golf course use a properly developed closeout system and not produce a positive response from the clients, employees and players. As a golf coach this is a checklist of sorts that you should have in your daily planner. You can go over it starting a couple of days before the closeout party to make sure you are successful.

One good closeout should represent about five days worth of revenue. One bad closeout is equal to five bad days. Be aware of this and make sure that you are set up and ready. Remember, golf clubs are about energy. The best operators are the ones that can create the energy, not only among the members and guests, but also among the staff. "Macy's white flower day," if you can tell me what a white flower day is, you are smarter than me.

The most successful day in retail store sales for many years was a closeout created by Macy's Department Store. It has nothing to do with anything other than a sale and the energy created by it.

A closeout in short is a party! A huge fiesta put together to create a buying frenzy. Most golf clubs will do the majority of the work for you and in mentioning work I am referring to the little things done by your golf course that build up the hype. It is still important to understand the process and do your part. All of the golf course passes (three and ten days) will expire or be extended on that day. All corporate open enrollment periods should be expiring that day. All special pricing will be expiring that day. One hundred "hot colored signs will be up in the club house, announcements are being made every 10 minutes, the telephone is answered in a different way and all schedules are cleared of member problems, golf lesson or one on one sessions.

Closeout is set up for selling only. Post-dated checks or credit cards should all be made for the 15th or the 30th of the month as this creates excitement among the staff. The contest box for the trip give-a-way should be front and center: The most important part about the trip give-a-way or the raffle is that you must be present to win. Also think about making a rule "bringing in a non-member is the only way to enter." The two most important elements of the party are the "raffle" in the evening or throughout the day and having several "outside vendors" coming in to promote their product. This will create a festive atmosphere in your golf club.

Make sure that all staff is at the club by 8:00 a.m., and that the club house is decorated by 9:00 a.m. Make sure to have one person scheduled to come in extremely early because there is a whole group of members and guests that like to come in early and you may miss an opportunity. You may be able to upgrade a training package or sell some personal coaching. The person that wants to make the biggest paycheck is probably the person that will be there early.

The Set Up

1. As you can see from the things I have listed above, the closeout set up starts from the beginning of the month. Developing good

Selling Golf

habits will ensure your success by following the points outlined above on a daily basis. The most important aspect of your personal performance on closeout will come from your ability to clear your schedule and book only handpicked orientation or sales opportunities. I like to hand pick my closeout orientations and I do this by having a free swing check testing booth set up a couple days prior to the party. I hand pick potential clients that seem interested. If they seem like they are interested in a one on one session, I book them for an appointment during our closeout party.

2. Each golf coach or training package pro should have a job assignment for the party. An example would be puting a coach in charge of setting up and running a supplement booth. Someone else may be in charge of making sure the club house is decorated with balloons. Another example would be to have one coach in charge of enrolling vendors to make the event more festive. The key to success will come from your team working from a plan.

3. Each coach should have approximately 15 orientations set. Those appointments should consist of 30 minute time periods and a goal for production should be set. These appointments should be confirmed and the confirmation call should include a brief explanation outlining the day's events.

4. 4. Each coach should call 50 current members and 50 missed guests to promote the closeout party. Call and leave messages and tell your potential clients and members about the opportunities, giveaways or even invite them to bring friends and families to train free of charge.

5. Signs must be up and the coaches, pros, the front desk staff and even the janitors should know the promotion. Have it planned and be sure to send out several confirmation calls. Have a production meeting with the staff or be involved in one so that every individual in the company is aware of the promotion and what the signs mean.

6. All "balance dues" and "promise to pays" must be collected or scheduled for closeout. Everyone that owes money should be

called and told to come in on closeout to pay their balance or they will be sent to collections.

7. Advise the front desk of telephone salutations and start it today. "Thank you for calling _____ on our closeout sale, how may I help you?" Promote whatever the special is when giving the telephone salutation and attach a copy of it to the telephone.

8. One pro should be working the front desk all day for "flips" and renewals. Make sure that one person is at the desk working check-ins and making sure that every person that walks in is told about the specials. This is a huge source of revenue for the company.

9. Before pros go home make sure that all appointments are written in the master appointment book.

10. All post dates should be put on the books and make sure to write them down the night before closeout. This way you know exactly how much needs to be made in order to hit your goal.

11. Spread the hype with each and every employee about the big day that is happening tomorrow. Make sure that everyone knows and understands what closeout is.

12. The country club should have a retail or sidewalk sale set up and they should handle any food, fashion shows or sidewalk sales. Coaches should be doing orientations, potential sales only and be in charge of supplement or golf seminars in the banquet room. Course marshals should clear their schedules and be in charge of course rules or strategy seminars. Golf coaches should do a golf seminar at some point in the evening or a golf exhibition out in front of the fairways.

13. Closeout should not cost the company money and should be part of the employee's job description. The staff will be getting paid extra commission based on the extra sales made. All trips, food and vendors should be traded out with the approval of the general manager or regional manager. No trade outs can be accepted for personal or staff use.

On the Day of Closeout

On the day of closeout you should have this list posted in your office and in your planner and you should make sure to do everything on the list.

1. On closeout, have a morning production meeting and motivate everybody. Get them excited. Let everyone know what is riding on the golf club's performance by highlighting where the golf course is at and what needs to be done in order to hit your goals.
2. Get balloons, streamers, and signs up so the golf course looks like there is a party going on.
3. Don't deal with any cancellations or customer service issues today. Today is pure production. No negativity is allowed.
4. Do 25 percent off retail and golf clubs and set up booths for the promotion of this such as, 'buy 2 get the 3rd one free' or 'buy 1 and get the 2nd for 50 percent off.'
5. Continue to promote the evening over the telephone.
6. No rounds for employees allowed on closeout.
7. Emphasize paid in full options. Every package should offer 1, 3 or 5 sessions free.
8. Make sure you have something to give-a-way to members. Do trade-outs with businesses to give away in a drawing on closeout. This creates a buying atmosphere.
9. Have an afternoon production meeting.
10. Nobody "walks" on closeout. Call your district manager to approve deals.
11. Dress in a different or new uniform. In my golf clubs I like to have a theme this gives the staff a chance to wear apparel of their choosing that coincides with the theme. Appearance and presence are half the battle.

Chapter 28

INTERACTING WITH THE STAFF

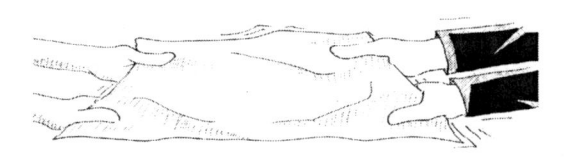

Staff interaction is an overlooked yet vital aspect of our business. Many golf coaches and course managers fail to do the groundwork and are unable to interact well with others. Loving your job or dreading the thought of even showing up to work could all depend on how well you work with your surrounding staff. Since we are in a commission driven business, coaches can become competitive. At times they will even cross the line of stealing or "sharking" packages. The way to handle these problems is quickly, privately and usually through your manager or club supervisor. Problems that are not handled immediately can fester into much larger problems that can affect the entire club.

Your manager

You golf course manager or club supervisor is the person who has the most to gain from your success in the golf course. At this level I can almost guarantee the managers are tied in to a piece of everything you sell, they truly have a vested interest in making sure that you are successful. I have found that many coaches being part time or being scheduled to work hours that do not always coincide with the management often become alienated from the people that are the true professionals in the club. Spend as much time as you can in an attempt to find out how these individuals think and what they want. Being in tune with the wants and needs of the person that hands out your pay check will increase your ability to grow and to learn from someone who has a proven track record in the industry. It is also important to understand that whenever there is a problem that concerns a new or important client, the manager is the one who will deal with it. In many cases these clients have had problems or need a new coach. Since they have usually spent (or spend) a lot of money on training, the manager will only hand out these clients to the coaches that they trust or have a good reputation for understanding the company systems.

Front desk

One of the most important relationships you can have will be with your front desk staff, as they are the first contact. They can control your paycheck.

One time I was upset because one of my important clients scheduled an early morning appointment on my day off of all things. I canceled a trip to meet with them and drove all the way to the club early in the morning only to find that the front desk person had not written down the message. My client had canceled the appointment many days prior. Being in a bad mood from the early wake up call I let this individual have it! Things really got ugly at that point and not only did I stop getting my messages but I found that my orientations were all kids with no money and people that had no interest in buying personal golf coaching. What I discovered is that these people actually recommend coaches to many of the players. I found that many of the potential clients interested in having a personal golf coaching would first ask the service desk staff which person they felt was the best coach.

Other coaches

Many of the coaches in the golf business today have a lot of knowledge on different aspects of golf technique. It has been through the relationships that I have built in the business that I have been able to keep my knowledge and skills sharp. I spend 2 hours a week making sure that I squeeze in a game with one of the other coaches. Ask questions, play together, trade clients, do sales role-playing and rely on them as sales professionals. This coach can answer a question about an area that is their specialty; this resource is at your fingertips. Use it and build a good relationship with your teammates.

Mentor

Not everyone starts off with great instincts when it comes to being a coach or the related sales process, but whatever abilities people have can be nurtured and developed. My first six months in a role where I was forced to sell personal golf coaching were very difficult. I felt that I was good with people but I did not have much in the way of natural sales ability. The system that I put together is geared towards people like myself: the 99 percent that are not gifted in sales. I feel that anyone can sell a package if they have the determination and ability to learn the system. There was no system when I started; it was just my mentor and I. He showed me his methods, he critiqued my weak points, gave me encouragement, TOed for me, helped me to understand the rules of the game and showed me the correct way to fill out a golf coaching agreement.

I owe most of my early success to my mentor. I probably would not have lasted as a coach if I hadn't had someone like this to help me. What did he gain in return? That is a simple answer. I worked on his team. If he needed to have someone stay late, or come in early, I was there. If he needed someone to work on Sunday, I was there. When he became a supervisor, I followed him to every golf course that he worked in. I followed out every task he asked down to the smallest detail. When he became a district director, he promoted me to manager and sent me to any country club that was doing poorly. I followed the system and increased sales in the low clubs so that they became the top clubs. Our relationship helped our company become more successful, and, in turn, we helped each other in becoming more successful. We made more money, because we worked together.

Sales

These are the guys you want to get in good with. In most cases the sales people in the golf club have access to the new members. The people that have just signed up are the best source of new clients. Building a good relationship with the sales department will put you in an ideal position to pick and choose the orientations that you feel have some interest in training or have some interest in you as their coach. As you build this symbolic relationship you may even find yourself being brought in to the sales process to T.O. for training or you may ask the help of the sales department for some help closing one of your clients! It is important to send any new sign ups for training packages to the sales person that is helping you and you will see a huge improvement in your training schedule

Increase Your Sales Knowledge

As the complete professional, you must continue to grow. You must improve your knowledge, your sales skills and your training information. Our business is a rapidly changing one. If you do not continue to grow, you will be left in the dust. The young people just starting in our business are at the top of their game. They are top athletes trained by the latest technology, and they know there is money to be made in our industry. They are hungry. There is a poster above my desk and it says,

"Every morning on the planes of Africa, the lion awakes, and knows it must outrun the slowest gazelle or it will starve to death. Every morning on the same plane, the gazelle awakes and knows it must outrun the fastest lion, or it will be killed." It does not matter if you are the lion or the gazelle. When you wake up in the morning, you'd better be running"

Selling Golf

We work in the one of the fastest growing industries in the world. Computerization has changed the amount of energy that we expel at work. By the year 2015, 25 percent of all Americans will be working from their homes. You literally will not even have to get up and walk in order to accomplish your job. The obesity rate is reaching staggering heights and the amount of information available about exercise and sports grows every day. Doctors are getting smarter, nutritionists are getter better, and golf equipment has improved dramatically. Let's face it: golf courses have come a long way from the old walk the whole course we used to have. The equipment used on the course like the ball and the clubs, even the golf bags have gone through a similar degree of change.

Mother Teresa of Calcutta quotes

If you are kind, people may accuse you of selfish, ulterior motives:
Be kind anyway.

People are often unreasonable, illogical and self-centered:
Forgive them anyway.

If you are successful, you will win some false friends and some true enemies:
Succeed anyway.

If you are honest and frank, people may cheat you:
Be honest and frank anyway.

What you spend years building, someone may destroy overnight:
Build anyway.

If you find serenity and happiness, they may be jealous:
Be happy anyway.

The good you do today, people will often forget tomorrow:
Do good anyway.

Give the world the best you have, and it may never be enough:
Give the world the best you have anyway

You see, in the final analysis, it is all between you and god:
It was never between you and them anyway.

Commissions.

The rules for splits and commissions can be at the forefront of many of the staff problems that arise in a golf clubs. It is important to lay down the ground rules for how to handle these sensitive issues. I suggest posting the rules so that every one is clear on how splits and other commissions work.

The interaction between sales and coaches can be a fine line of controversy so the rule that we have used for splits is the following. A T.O. should never be split. If a coach conducts a T.O. for a sales person or a sales person does a T.O. for a coach, the original person should receive all the commission. New coaches will not T.O. if they have to split their deals. (A supervisor or manager should generally do a T.O.) If a coach has an appointment for a training package, it is an appointment and should be split with the coach. The coach must have the appointment in the book or in their planner. If you have a person come back to the golf course, and it is not in the MAB and they do not ask for you, it is not yours. If a walk in asks for someone one it is an ask-for or an appointment, and should be split if it is taken by someone other than the requested person. If a sales person sells a package, that commission goes entirely to the sales person. A package sold by the sales department should be given to the club director for coaching allocation. The sales staff counselor can only sign up a member on a training package if; #1 The member has never bought P.C. #2 The member has a package that has been expired for more than a month. #3 At the point of sale on a new training package. Coaches should let the members know that if they are interested in any golfing programs they should go through them and can specify that this is how they earn a living. Last but not least, orientations go to the coaches.

These are just some of the rules we run at our clubs. We have used these rules for years, and they work very well. Remember, what goes around comes around. If you are not consistent, you will run into problems, in which case remember to handle your issues immediately and fairly. You may even consider posting the rules, so that everybody is clear on them. In one of the clubs I worked in, the manager had the sales staff vote on each rule, he then posted the rules on the wall and we never had a problem.

Negativity is the cancer that ruins your paycheck. Do not get caught up in other people's business. Mom always says, "Mind your own business." Remember, if you have complaints or something negative to say, complaints go up. Complaints don't go level or down, they go up. Keep focused on your business at hand, stay away from the fun bunch and have clear rules of commission. Stay on the good side of all the departments, attend meetings, and follow your to-do list every single day. By following simple rules of staff interaction, you will truly love your job in the golf industry.

Chapter 29

GIVING A FREE GIFT WITH PURCHASE

I don't know why, but the old free gift with purchase gets them every time, just ask the department stores. They have made millions of dollars in their cosmetic departments just by offering a free gift along with the purchase of a package. I have had good success with three different options in reference to a free gift with purchase.

1. The first option that has worked well for our company has also been used to generate interest in almost all of the companies that I have worked for. It is a very simple process, basically if a player enrolls in the starter package, they will receive a limited time prize. For instance, "enroll in the starter package between now and the end of the month and receive a free Sony Walkman. This offer expires 11/30/2004." You can do the same for the accelerated result package. Get started on the accelerated result package between now and the end of the month and receive a free LV wallet. When I use the free gift with purchase program, I only use the item available for about a five-day period and I rarely use the same item twice. Many of these items may be purchased for a discount or a partial trade for a training package. Remember to ensure your manager has approved all trade outs!

2. The second option has also been used to provide outstanding results and to create urgency at the end of the month. The process for offering the free gift with purchase comes in the form of a larger prize and depends on the amount of sessions that are purchased, you will receive one entry for each session. So

Selling Golf

for example, a client enrolls in the starter package and receives six entries whereas a client that purchases 32 sessions would have 32 entries in the drawing. Once again to create urgency, the drawing is held on closeout and the only people who are invited to participate in this drawing are those who enrolled in the one on one program during the competition dates.

3. The third option is where you have a contest or a challenge that includes a set amount of sessions and a prize for the winner of the challenge. So for instance, the program may require each contestant to complete 32 sessions of personal golf coaching in a 60-day period. Based on the evaluation results taken at the end of the 60-day period prizes can be given to the top three contestants. As an extra incentive you may wish to offer a free T-shirt to anyone who participates.

Chapter 30

CONFIRMING APPOINTMENTS AND CANCELLATIONS

There are three ways you can operate in a Country Club.
1. You can get setup and get prepared.
2. You can wait for walk-ins.
3. You can pray!

If you have been a coach for any period of time, you will find yourself in situations where you have the devil on your left shoulder and an angel on your right shoulder. You will be sitting in front of a check with your name on it and a client who is happy to deliver another large package. As you wipe the beads of sweat from your forehead, the words are going through your mind, "Should I or shouldn't I?" Another twenty hours spent in anguish over a client who takes advantage of my generosity and hard work.

We talked earlier about the difference between loving your day-to-day life as a career golf coach and dreading the next re-enrollment. It all depends on your ability to keep a healthy relationship with your trade and your client base. Loving your job or dreading the thought of even showing up to work can all depend on how well you establish boundaries with your clients. When it comes to rescheduling and cancellation of appointments, I try to set down the rules for what is and is not acceptable and what it will cost per session.

On the following page are some of the rules we run at our golf courses. We have used these rules for years and they have worked very well for us. If you do not practice consistency it is likely that you will run into problems.

Always remember to handle your issues immediately and consistently. You may even consider posting the rules, so that everybody is clear on them. You can also have your clients sign a waiver that has all the rules listed so that there are no misunderstandings and then post the rules on the wall. We never had problems in the past when doing this as the client is left unable to feign ignorance. The confirmation box will allow you make a note if the appointment has been confirmed. I like to call my appointments from home just to confirm that they are coming in before I leave for the golf course. Also, it is important to call and check the book to see if any new appointments have been scheduled for the day. Your personal golf clients should have access to your voicemail system so they can call if they have any last minute cancellations.

Agreement for personal golf coaching guidelines

1. All personal golf sessions must be made or rescheduled 24 hours prior to the appointment time. Training sessions that are not cancelled in advance may still incur a charge. All clients are responsible for having the direct phone line or message center to their particular coach. Messages left at the front desk or at the corporate office may not reach coaches in time to be considered 24 hour advanced notice.

2. #1 Golf Club golf coaches have hourly coaching appointments. Please be aware that if you are late, irrespective of your session start time, your coach must finish on time and not run over.

3. As a #1 Golf Club member, you agree to the time limit in which the personal coaching package must be completed. If extra time is required to complete the package, this extension must be approved by the #1 Golf Club corporate office.

4. All personal coaching clients must agree to a physical examination prior to starting a personal coaching program. The client is responsible for making sure they are physically fit to exercise.
5. #1 Golf Club has agreed to provide a coach for the sessions indicated. #1 Golf Club does not agree to make all of your sessions completed with the same coach.
6. The client agrees to notify #1 Golf Club if at any time they are not comfortable with the personal golf coach they are working with. Clients may change coaches at any time. The client also agrees to notify #1 Golf Club of any extended leave.

Client: _____ Coach: _____

Chapter 31

DRILLING

Repetition is the mother of learning and the father of action, which makes it the architect of accomplishment

Drilling is an essential part of the human behavioral learning process. Repetition is the key to perfection. Every time we do something we get a little better at it and it gradually becomes easier and easier until we reach a point where we can do it without thinking, this is the place that we long to be. The unconscious competence: You don't have to think about riding a bike, and you don't have to think about catching a ball. You don't have to think about walking. But all of these things at one point in our life were difficult. It took a lot of effort and practice to perfect these simple things. Selling is just as easy as riding a bike, although it may not seem so to a beginner. Most people at the age of five learn to ride a bike. They don't learn to sell. A professional football player practices throwing a football every day of his life and still continues to practice every day once he gets in the pros. All-professional's drill: boxers, basketball players, racecar drivers, doctors and lawyers. *Practice, practice, practice, drill, drill, drill.*

Mirroring and Matching Drill

This drill requires two golf coaches sitting face to face mirroring and matching every movement. You want to focus on the energy, the breathing, everything involved in mimicking the person to a "T".

The Question Game

The question game is a simple but effective way to learn the art of selling. This technique has been instrumental in my ability to train top-notch golf sales professionals. Answering a question with a question and staying calm under fire is at the heart of what selling is all about. It took me a long time to develop a drill that could teach the fundamentals that were the real difference between a new sales person and a seasoned one. One day it dawned on me that the difference between a new sales person and a seasoned one was as simple as the experienced sales person knowing how to ask questions instead of answering them. This is the little or **big** difference in communication styles! This drill helped put the sales person in control of the conversation thus enabling them to control the thoughts of the player through a series of questions. When each of the questions is asked, the player needs time to think of the answer and the sales process begins. This drill is my invention and I have never seen it used in any other publication. To perform the drill, sit across from another coach and ask them a question. The other coach (in a role playing manner), will then answer with a question, to which you will reply with another question and so forth.

Example;

Golf Coach 1: How much does it cost for a training package?

Golf Coach 2: Were you looking for a training package for yourself, a family or a couple?

Golf Coach 1: Do you have any golf classes?

Golf Coach 2: What kind of golf classes are you interested in?

Golf Coach 1: Do you have a driving range?

Golf Coach 2: Were you interested in a training package with driving practice or just a training package today?

Golf Coach 1: What time is the club the busiest?

Golf Coach 2: What time will you be using the club most?

The Tough Customer Drill

This is a great drill for new coaches that want to become better at selling. You have to learn to be direct and to come back at your guest with the same energy they are giving you. This is not the time to back down. Your potential client is trying to take control, this is their technique. This is the time for you to take control by matching the abrasiveness brought on by the client.

Closing Drill

In a role-playing situation, try to overcome objections given by your club supervisor or another coach. Ask your partner, "If I can get you a great deal on a training package, would you want to get started today?" Have your partner respond by saying, "Not today, maybe, I want to try it first, I would consider it, and no." Drill on overcoming these objections. You may try "if it was $10 per session, would you be able to make a decision to get started on the program today?" Also drill on "out of the different package options, which one are you leaning towards?" Your partner would respond with the seven common objections. "I want to think about it!" "I need to speak to my spouse." "It is too much money." Use the steps outlined in overcoming objections. Practice overcoming five objections, and make sure your partner is being realistic: not too hard, and not too easy.

Filling Out the Personal Coaching Agreement Drill

This could be one of the most important drills. Most of the personal coaching deals that are lost are done so the moment the agreement comes out. Objections start to flow the moment the pen tries to touch the paper. Filling out the contract is the pivotal moment where most new golf coaches will lose their potential client or miss their sales. First try practicing by using stalling tactics. Pretend that you are a potential client and try grabbing the personal coaching agreement. Practice by answering questions with questions or by tapping your finger at the signature spot. You could try bringing up objections over paying with a credit card and even about payment method or type. You can also mention wanting to return at a later time to pay. If you can master through drilling, the ability to control your potential client during this most important time in the sales process, you will find this will highly increase your closing percentages.

Personal Coaching Presentation

Practice your P.C. presentation until you have learned it word for word. Drill on difficult, detailed questions on golf technique that your guest may ask. Your presentation should sound smooth and unrehearsed. You should practice being an empathetic listener and your presentation should leave clients truly understanding the value of the program that you are offering to them. Remember; "practice makes perfect!"

Setting up a Free Coaching Session or Orientation

Repetition is the mother of learning and the father of action, which makes it the architect of accomplishment. When establishing a successful personal coaching program, the first step in your success will be filling up your orientation book. Having quality opportunities is the key to any successful business. Drilling on overcoming objections to the free lesson is important. You will hear statements such as, "I will try it on my own," You may even hear, "I don't need a coach." Overcoming these objections will help you keep your book full and confirm future success.

Chapter 32

THE SALES PROFESSIONAL CODE

As the complete sales professional it is important to grade yourself in an honest manner. Self-reflection is a way of making sure that the product that you are selling remains the primary focus. As you grow and fully understand the sales process you will begin to internalize and understand that in most cases the product that you are selling is *you*. Once you understand this rule, you will begin to develop a system of improving the product. Below I have outlined a detailed code of daily affirmation. This will aid in creating a healthy relationship between your trade and your life.

1. I am human and I am a slave to my daily routine.

    My daily routine attacks my free will, due to years of accumulative habits and the past deeds of my life. I have already marked a path which threatens to imprison my future. My actions are ruled by my appetite, passion, prejudice, greed, love, fear, environment, and habit. And the worst of these tyrants is habit. I will form good habits and become their slave.

2. I will greet this day with love in my heart.

    My reasoning they may counter; my speech they may distrust; my apparel they may disapprove; my face they may reject; and even my bargains may cause them suspicion; yet my love will melt all hearts, likened to the sun whose rays soften the coldest clay.

3. I will persist until I succeed.

    I am a lion and I refuse to talk, to walk, or to sleep with the sheep. I will hear not those who are weak and complain, for their disease is contagious. Let them join the sheep. The slaughter house of failure is not my destiny. The prizes of life are at the end of each journey, not near the beginning.

4. I am nature's greatest miracle.

I am rare, and there is value in all rarity; therefore, I am valuable. I am the end product of thousands of years of evolution; therefore, I am better equipped in both mind and body than all the emperors and wise men that preceded me.

5. I will live this day as if it is my last.

I will waste not a moment moaning yesterday's misfortune, yesterday's defeat, yesterday's heartache, for why should I throw away good after that. This is my day to excel.

6. Today I will be the master of my emotions.

I will learn this secret of the ages: Weak is he who permits his thoughts to control his actions; strong is he who forces his actions to control his thoughts. *Each day, when I awaken, I will follow this plan of battle before I am captured by the forces of sadness, self-pity and failure.*

7. I will laugh at the world.

I will laugh at my failures and they will vanish in clouds of new dreams; I will laugh at my success and they will shrink to their true value. I will laugh at evil and it will die untested; I will laugh at goodness and it will thrive and abound. Each day will be triumphant only when my smiles bring forth smiles.

8. Today I will multiply my value a hundredfold.

I will set goals for the day, the week, the month, the year, and my life. Just as the rain must fall before the wheat will crack its shell and sprout, so must I have objectives before my life will crystallize. In setting my goals I will consider my best performance of the past and multiply it a hundredfold.

9. I will act now.

My dreams are not worthy. My plans are nothing and my goals are impossible. All are of no value unless they are followed by action. Action is the good and the drink which will nourish my success. I must always act without hesitation and the flutters in my heart will vanish.

10. I shall have faith in my higher power.

Never will I seek delivery of gold, love, good health, pretty victories, fame, success, or happiness. Only for guidance will I pray that I may be shown the way to acquire these things, and my prayers will always be answered. The guidance I seek may come, or the guidance I seek may not come, but are not both of these an answer? I will pray for guidance.

OG MANDINO

Chapter 33

TO SELL OR NOT TO SELL

To sell or not to sell, that is the question. Recently, we have been hearing the faint whispers of a growing number of business professionals blaming the sales process as the smoking gun for all of the shortcomings in our industry. This negative force has been deemed the reason for some kind of slow growth. When putting some deep thought into this important issue we must look at our industry and we must look into the future as well as into the past. The first question I ask is "**what** slow growth?" The golf business next to the size of the McDonalds or Coke may be the fastest growing thing on the planet. Due to the present down turn in the economy most companies within our core markets failed to survive. While all the other businesses are thinking of ways to improve and enhance the sales process we are thinking of abandoning it.

The shortcomings that we have are a staple in any growing business. Ours comes not from the selling process but more from the lack of getting all of our ships to sail in the same direction. Not in the selling process but in the professional level, or lack thereof, which our industry requires for training and keeping a mature staff. Selling is a tool and nothing more, *should the chef stop creating his mastery's in the kitchen because he is burned by the flame or blame the knife for a nick on the finger?*

Selling Golf

Selling is a tool and when used properly it may be referred to as the greatest profession ever created by man! However, it is a very powerful and complicated tool; when used properly it can be extremely effective and when used carelessly it can be dangerous. Studied in depth it is as powerful and infinite as the human mind and yet it is also as basic in human nature as children's first questions. I agree our process must evolve and it will, but it must do so without abandoning the knowledge gained by our predecessors.

We must understand that we are dealing with people as our product. We sell dreams and results and sometimes failure, thus we must endeavor to understand that each and every client is different. We must also accept that the incredible growth of our industry could be called the most explosive business invention of the century.

To those who say this industry and its systems are not extraordinary and that growth means the abandonment of competition, victory and selling dreams, I say never.

Made in the USA